RICH

girl

POOR

girl

RICH
girl

POOR
girl

HOW TO BECOME THE RICH GIRL
YOU WERE ALWAYS MEANT TO BE

PAM SOWDER

Clovercroft Publishing

Published by Clovercroft Publishing, Franklin, Tennessee

Edited by OnFire Books

Copy edit by Adept Content Solutions

Cover and Interior Design by Adept Content Solutions

Printed in the United States of America

Hard cover ISBN 978-1-950892-67-9

Trade paperback ISBN 978-1-954437-06-7

Contents

"So, I tell you: Ask and it will be given to you; seek and you will find; knock and the door will be opened to you."
—LUKE 11:9

Dedication

To my parents, Barbara and Gene, thank you for always believing in me even when you thought I was crazy.

To my husband, Dave, who loves me no matter what and gives so much to our family with his generous and kind spirit.

To my son Adam, who has taught me that with darkness there will be light, and it is by living through Jesus Christ.

To my daughter, Kaye, who lights up my world with her huge heart and profound love for me.

To my son-in-law, Scott, thank you for asking provocative questions that keep me on my toes.

To my son Inguss from a different mother, thank you for always making me feel so loved and special.

To my grandchildren, Kennedy and Miles, thank you for allowing me to be your Mimi. I love you both with all my heart and soul.

To Elvis, thank you for the joy.

To you my family and friends, thank you for believing in me as much as I believe in you.

Thank you to Mark Pentecost & the It Works Family for being such a blessing not only for me and my family but for countless thousands who want more in life in the way of friendships, fun and freedom.

Foreword

Often, we judge people, an industry, a book by its cover, but if we explore and ask questions, we find that they are very different than what we first thought or imagined. It is my wish that you will explore the network marketing industry, as I did in 1994, and look at the possibilities that it can give you. It has been a gift. A most treasured one that continues to give and I continue to unwrap. The gifts have been way more than monetary; they have been gifts of friendship, fun, and freedom. A life filled with hopes, dreams, and endless possibilities: a life that has challenged me to grow, sometimes more than I was willing. I started for the money, and I'll continue for the gifts that I will more than likely never stop unwrapping. I am now the Rich Girl who feels so blessed that she can seize life with the understanding that being rich in life is what God intended. May you have an open mind to explore this industry that never stops giving.

Introduction

Do you desire to be the rich girl—the girl who has a loving family, heartfelt friendships, the happiness of living a full and enriched life that is so fun and creative that you can't wait to get up in the morning? How about a prosperous business that gives you such tremendous joy and energy that every day feels like a new day of experiences while having the ability to create unlimited income? I wanted to be that girl, and I was willing to fight for her because I once remembered those little girl dreams, those dreams that over decades got lost. I grew up knowing that I could be that girl, but I let people, circumstances, and my own disbelief in myself stand in the way.

I love my family, and while I was blessed to be a stay-at-home mom, I felt unfulfilled at times, lonely, and missed adult interaction, plus I wanted to be able to contribute financially to our family that had growing needs. I felt and thought like a poor girl, a girl who wanted more but felt trapped by traditions that caused me to feel depressed at times and then guilty for feeling that way. I would continually ask myself, "What is wrong with you? You have it all." But I knew I didn't in some ways, and I didn't know what was missing until I found my way out. You see, I missed building something for myself. I missed being in the marketplace—the excitement of what the world has to offer. I missed being able to purchase gifts for my husband and friends without having to ask my husband for money. I missed the freedom to create without feeling guilty about it. I now know that I was feeling poor in spirit and I was always thinking about what was not working for me that everyone else deserves it but me, that I might not be smart enough, strong enough, or lucky enough, much less deserving enough. These are the thoughts of lack, limitation, and just plain stinking thinking. These are the thoughts of a poor girl.

My husband, Dave, aka Big Daddy, has always been an incredible provider, a wonderful husband, and father who wanted everything for his family; however, he was feeling the stress of being the only financial provider. He started suggesting that I get a job, which was like a four-letter word to me. Seriously, it made me sick to my stomach thinking about leaving our children with a sitter or an after-school program. I continued to avoid the subject until I no longer could and had to face the facts. I needed to find work. I struggled looking for a job because of the demands that I knew it would place on our family. This story is about finding that solution to living each day feeling like I could breathe, that I could contribute but still stay home and work part-time, or more time if I chose to. It's not the traditional way of doing business, but I have found for me and my family it worked, and it worked big-time. I hope that you too will find within these pages a new way of looking at a business model that is for most people taboo or has "scam" seemingly written all over it. However, it helped take this poor girl's life and turn it into a rich girl's fairytale: a life of passion, compassion, friendships all over the world, a family rich with memories of an entrepreneurial mom who was still there to raise her children while building a legacy. Rich is way beyond the millions that this life has provided us and more about our life of being a family that has learned so much about who we are and where we can go. I want that for you, that girl or guy who wants more in life. It is my wish that you find out who you really are and what you are capable of. This was and still is the best school for life, you learn everything about yourself, and as we say in our industry, "This is a self-development course for living a big life with an opportunity wrapped around it." Let's get over ourselves and start to understand that we have an opportunity for growth on all levels that is limitless. And, don't forget one of the most important elements: it must be FUN!

Chapter 1

Uncovering Your Why

"What you want, wants you."
—PAM SOWDER

What's your why? Don't know yet? That's okay. Let's uncover it together.

It can seem like an overwhelming question, or perhaps you might be thinking, "Why is my *why* so important?" Your why is the thing that makes you laugh and cry, almost within the same breath once you allow it in; it's the thing that drives you to get out of bed in the morning with excitement and expectancy—that honeymoon feeling. Remember that? That sexy, powerful feeling of living in the moment. You couldn't get out of bed fast enough, and the entire world looked brighter. Everyone around you was happy but especially you. You were deeply and profoundly in love. You had the feeling that something big was about to happen. According to Dr. Bruce Lipton, it is "a state of bliss, passion, energy, and health resulting from a huge love. Your life is so beautiful that you can't wait to get up to start a new day and you are so thankful that you are alive." Your why is the catalyst that casts the vision, that gives you that crystal clear picture of what you want.

My rich girl why is absolutely different from my poor girl why. My poor girl why was about getting by, doing less, blame, living in fear, and regret. My rich girl why is about abundance, creativity, wisdom, living in the moment, and knowing that more is worth going after.

If you are building a business and a new life, knowing your why is crucial. It not only keeps you going, but it gets you through the roughest parts of building a business. Your why is a guiding light that keeps you focused and on track professionally and personally.

How do you find your why? I found mine by going back in time and looking at what I loved doing as a child and what I loved to play. I loved to play school and play the part of the teacher. I can still picture myself, gathering all the things I needed to teach my "class:" pencils and books, setting up a chalkboard, chairs, and gathering anything that I could think of to make sure that I'd get my friends and siblings to play school with me. I owe my younger brother, Brian, so much because I would always make him sit and play with me. It was just who I was before I was even thinking about who I wanted to be when I grew up. I graduated from college with a degree in business education because I knew that was my calling; however, teaching took a different direction that I or anyone else could have possibly imagined.

I also loved playing Barbie dolls with my sister, Terry. We would play for hours. We would design clothes for Barbie from the Sears catalog, and Mom, who was an amazing seamstress, would take remnants of leftover fabric while we watched her in awe as she sewed those pieces of fabric into clothes. I had a passion for designing and seeing those designs come to life along with all the shoes and handbags that Barbie had. Barbie was styling! This is one of the reasons that I also wanted to earn my own money. I loved the latest looks in fashion from an early age, but that required money, and at the time we didn't have very much coming in. My dad worked during the day as a programmer for the railroad and at night he worked at Sears so that we could get clothes and gifts at a discount. I remember each school year my sister and I could pick out six dresses each for $36, and because we were thirteen months apart, we could wear the same clothes, so we combined those dresses into twelve and would wear one every two weeks. Once Mom started sewing, we could get more creative with our school clothes, and that started me on the path of fashion.

Think about what you really loved doing when you were a child, and like me it could be multiple things. Be quiet and really dig into your memories. What were the games you would play and who would you pretend to be? It can seem like a cliché when people say, "Do what you love, and you will never have to work a day in your life," but what would you do if you suddenly had a windfall of money, didn't have to worry about bills, and didn't have to work a job?

What would a day in your life look like if you weren't spending all your time on the daily grind? It is an important question and, for many, one that is difficult to answer and that they are not even willing to ask themselves. What do you do when you're just being you, and no one is telling you what you should do? If you could do or have anything, what would it be? We don't often ask ourselves questions like this, but we should! Allow your imagination to run wild. What would your day look like in this vision? Once you've got that vision in your mind, hang on to it. You're going to use it to develop your why and to create your day.

Before discovering the network marketing industry, I was looking for a way to be able to stay at home with my kids while working in the pockets of time throughout the day. I honestly didn't care what I did, I just wanted and very much needed to bring some extra cash in without putting on pantyhose, getting in the car, and going to a job. Can you relate? Maybe not with the pantyhose! When you think about your day, think about how your day would start and how it would end. What would the moments in between look like?

In my case, I needed flexibility in making a little extra cash to take the financial stress off myself and Dave. His job was very demanding as he worked long hours, and most nights he was out of town. In other words, I didn't see how a 9 to 5 schedule could work for me. I wanted to be able to manage my time, my way. I think often that this is what many people are after—time. They often think it's money they want, but what they are really yearning for is freedom to control their time. Time is the one thing we can never get back, and the freedom to choose how I was using mine was invaluable to me.

Dave is the practical one in the family. He was thinking job, and I was thinking, "Is there a way to work but not work?" which made zero sense to most people, including Dave. It was a real fear for me, this job thing. I know the same is true for many moms out there. Now, if you are a mom who loves the thought of going to work everyday, there's no judgment about that, if that is what you want; however, for me it was not an option that I could conceive of, much less consider.

While being a stay-at-home mom is a very fulfilling experience, there's a side effect for some women like myself who feel that they've lost themselves. Most of us want to be all in as parents; however, it is easy to allow motherhood to become our identity, which can later feel like a trap. I started to feel more and more disconnected from the dreams that I had as a young girl. I loved my children as much as any parent but grew bored with doing the same thing day after day, especially when they went off to school. You are so busy when they are little that you don't have much time to think, but as they enter school, you start asking questions such as, "Who am I? What am I supposed to do now? Have I lost my mojo? Can I get it back? Has my brain turned to mush? Am I still valuable? Can I even think? Who would want someone my age (and we are still so dang young)?" These are the thoughts of the poor girl.

So, how do we uncover this deep-seated "Why?" Once again, go back in time. Give yourself the time to really ask yourself some big questions. Don't think about anyone or anything else. This is an important first step in beginning this new life that you want. Don't be afraid of wanting something bigger for yourself. Don't be afraid of hurting someone because you want more. After discovering what I truly wanted in my life, everyone else was happier too. I wanted a big life filled with anticipation, love, creativeness, gratitude, endless possibilities along with zest and full on fun, loads of laughter and surprises. Bring me the miracles. I am ready.

ASK YOURSELF:

Have you lost yourself?

Do you feel as though you are living for everyone else and not for yourself?

Do you miss true connections with people?

Do you miss that girl who dreamed big dreams?

What skills and dreams did you have as a kid that you've lost touch with?

Are you looking for a job but secretly don't want one?

Or, would you rather have time and freedom that allows you to earn money on your terms?

Ask yourself these questions as you continue to read, and keep a notebook by your side so you can write down your thoughts as they come to you. The answers will become your why.

Chapter 2

Oh No, Not One of Those Things

"It's not normal, but it works."
—PAM SOWDER

I remember our first network marketing meeting. Dave and I really didn't want to be there. We went because one of Dave's best customers invited us, so I thought that both of us should go out of a sense of obligation. Never in my wildest dreams did I know what we were about to walk into—a moment in time that would change the trajectory of our lives forever. I've since learned that sometimes the best opportunities come when we are in search of something, but life decides to deliver it to us in a completely different package than what we expected. I had no idea that this meeting would change my perspective about an industry that I knew very little about or that I would gain a new career path.

As you can imagine, and maybe you have felt this way too, I thought meetings like this were a waste of time and a scam and somewhat cheesy. Losing several hours of my evening when I had things to do such as look for a job that I didn't want was frustrating, and it put me in that negative mindset of being completely closed off to the prospect of what I could learn, which is typical of how a poor girl thinks: mostly of herself and not open to a new way of working or an opportunity.

As we sat in a classroom at a local college and listened to a presentation, my arms were crossed, and all I could think about were the kids and what Dave and I were going to have for dinner later. The presenter was way too excited about what he was sharing. He had one of those old-fashioned flip charts, which was massive—about the same size that he was. He had a $100 bill that he kept sticking to his forehead as he spoke; it kept falling off because he was jumping around so much with such pure raw excitement. Look, that's not normal. Most meetings are boring, and the presenter makes you fall asleep. He was anything but boring—way too darn excited. It was both a turnoff and a turn-on at the same time. So, I was only half paying attention when something he said finally caught my attention. He said, "Now, if you get a few who get a few to try the service then you can earn *residual income and that can be while you are sleeping.*" I bolted upright in my chair and thought, "Wait a minute, what do you mean…you get money even when you're sleeping?"

Residual income, a term that everyone should understand.

Have you had those defining moments when something that seemed impossible started to look as if it could be possible? I was about to learn that there was an industry out there that could change my life.

It blew me away to learn that you could build an organization with family, friends, and people that you haven't met yet, that you could set your own hours: part-time, full-time, or whatever you wanted, and that you could earn residual income. After the meeting, as Dave and I sat at the restaurant that's all I could think and talk about—working from home and somehow earning residual income, along with the endless possibilities for making money. I went to bed that night and hardly slept. How could I? I had been distressed that I was going to lose the chance to stay home with our children, but instead I was looking now at an opportunity to change our family's financial life without the constraints of someone else's schedule!

The next morning, after such a fitful but hopeful sleep, I got up early with anticipation and curiosity. I put the kids in the car and drove straight to the library. Yes, I said the library. Back in 1994 there was no Google, so I had to do my research the old-fashioned way: with books and articles. I checked out books on the network marketing industry and multilevel marketing (MLM) and quickly devoured them. Instead of jumping in headfirst and doing it, I wanted to know whether it was a legitimate way to earn money. I even called the company that they were talking about, and when they picked up the phone, I hung up. Okay, they are real. You know the adage, "If it seems too good to be true, do your research!" I knew if I wanted to find my way to freedom, I needed to do some research and due diligence.

There were several network marketing companies that I already knew of. Avon and Tupperware were the first two that came to mind as I'd been to parties with my mom when I was little, but I didn't really understand how those worked.

Until the night of that meeting, the whole concept was totally off my radar. When I began to do my research, I saw, for the first time, that perhaps this was the vehicle for making money I'd dreamed of growing up. Today, there are many names for the industry: direct sales, network marketing, social selling, or influencer marketing. It doesn't matter which name it goes by, when you are ready to step out of your comfort zone and pursue your dreams, you will see that this industry creates freedom for those who are truly ready for it.

For me, I'd never been so excited about a potential opportunity in my life. The ability to work my own hours while at home, to go after the check that I wanted to make, and to have the flexibility to travel with my husband and kids was unknown to me until this defining moment. It was an opportunity that I couldn't pass by. With my research backing me, I was ready to dive in and get started, or so I thought. My sponsor was consistent at following up with me and asking me if I was ready to start. Multiple times I said no, but several months after that first meeting, I said, "Yes, let's do this." I was finally ready to make the commitment, so I joined. I paid $599 to join a company out of pure faith, and believe me, this money was in our savings account and meant a lot to us, so I needed to make sure I would earn it back quickly. I was so ready, or at least I thought I was. However, something unexpected happened the minute the check went in the mail, and that was paralyzing *fear*, a gripping heart-stopping fear seized me and took over my mind. I started to ask myself questions such as, "What if I fail?" "What if nobody buys from me?" "What if I do recruit some people; then what?" And the biggie, "What are people going to think?"

I can't explain this fear, but it stopped me for six solid months. I kept researching, I kept waiting for it to go away, and my husband kept asking me, along with my sponsor, "When are you going to get started?" I didn't even know what to tell them, because I was too embarrassed to tell them that I was scared.

One day my sponsor called and said the following month one of the top income earners would be two hours away and speaking at a meeting. He said he was a former teacher and had two kids just like me. He said he was from the south just like me. He said that I could relate to him and his story, but that I needed to hear it myself. Something told me to go, so I drove the two hours by myself because I still had not told anyone what I was doing. I sat in the back of that room and heard his story, and something within me came alive—that same feeling I had at the first meeting I attended but more intense. Hearing his story made me feel that if he could do it, so could I. He was making well over a million a year, and I would be overjoyed at $1,000 per month.

After he spoke, I waited in line to meet him. As I shook his hand, he asked me how I was doing. I started making up all kinds of excuses, and he saw right through me. He took a step back and placed one hand on his hip and looked me dead in the eye and said, "You are just too prissy for this!" Now, in the south that means you think you are too good for this, and boy, did he nail me. I had an aha moment, and it seemed as though time had stopped. I did think that, and that was why I was placing so much emphasis on what others would think and not on what our family needed.

I cried all the way home—deep sobbing cries—and with those tears came a resolve, a resolve to get started. The next morning, I woke up early and made a list of contacts. I started calling off that list and asking them to meet with me. I called my mom and said, "Mom, you are going to be my customer." I said it with such power and authority that she and so many others said, *Yes!* I got some no's too, but I didn't let them bother me. I knew that they didn't know what I knew. I kept going. I hosted our first meeting, and someone joined. I was off and running; however, I was just beginning this amazing journey. All along, I had my why, but it wasn't enough until I heard his story because I could relate to him, and I felt that if he could do it, so could I. That is why to this day I have learned to become a great storyteller—the teller of my stories and countless others.

I'll never forget my first check in the first month after I got started after those fearful first six months was for $15.78. That made it tangible. It was real—not a scam, and not a gimmick. The potential was there for me to bring in income! The second month my check was $203, and by the third month I was up to $748. My goal was to earn $1000 a month, and when I got there, my sponsor inspired me to go for more. It had never dawned on me to try to earn more than $1000 a month, so I accepted the challenge, and the next month my check was $2300. After that, it jumped to $4000. What's the difference between earning $15 and $4000 a month? It's belief and the willingness to go after your dreams with a mindset that knows it is possible. As I stated earlier, it didn't occur to me to go beyond the $1000 per month goal that I had set for myself until I was asked about why I didn't go for more. Once I realized within that 60-second conversation that it was something I could go after, I did. I didn't have to think deeply about it because I realized I was already doing what it would take to get there. I've learned to continue to ask myself, "Why not go for more?" and to not be afraid of it or overthink it.

ASK YOURSELF:

What are your current thoughts about network marketing?

Have you ever thought about working from home?

What would your life be like if you could?

Are you happy with your current job situation or business? If not, what is holding you back from going after what you want?

What steps would you need to take to leave your comfort zone and change your future?

Are you willing to open your mind and your heart to think about the possibilities that this industry could bring you?

Chapter 3

Days Lead to Weeks, to Months, to Years

"Love the life you have while you create the life of your dreams."
—HAL ELROD

Once I got started building and working with a team, I realized many challenges that would take place along the way, and these next few chapters talk about those challenges and the things that I have had to learn to overcome and embrace them. But what kept me going in the best of times and the worst of times was always wanting each day to play out in a way that made life worth waking up to.

Remember in the first chapter when I asked you what you loved doing as a child? It's still within you waiting to come alive. Be very still. Get in touch with your inner child. You know who she is. The one with the dream. The one who gets a glimpse of what it would be like to wake up each day doing the things that you love doing. I would highly recommend that you ask yourself what it is you really want and what would make you feel vibrant and full of inspiration. Journal these thoughts that are coming through and pay close attention to how you feel.

Imagine what your everyday life would look like if you were doing the things that you loved and that money was no longer occupying most of your thoughts, and when you thought of money it would be with a deep appreciation and an exhilaration of knowing that you are creating exactly what you want. What would it be like to wake up in the morning at whatever time you wanted because you couldn't wait to get up? You didn't need an alarm because you knew that the day was yours, that you were truly living in it and loving every minute of it, that the day would flow and that there is true happiness in it.

Do you currently get up with an alarm clock, rush through the morning, rush to work, don't take lunch, rush home only to start a second shift with tons more to accomplish before you drop exhausted into bed knowing that tomorrow will be the same? Before you know it, ten years have gone by, then twenty, and nothing has changed. There is nothing wrong with this if this is all you can see for yourself, but there is a world of opportunities, and I wanted those opportunities and life for myself and my family. It is the life of the rich girl.

What if you could take your days and life back by giving yourself permission to live your days your way? I'd like to challenge you to take the time to start writing out a plan for what you feel what be the perfect day for you. Start writing down thoughts and ideas as you go about your day and how you would like it to be instead of what you are currently experiencing. Become very aware of what your day really feels like as you go through it. The emotions that you feel are very important to this process. I will give you more details on how to do this in chapter 5, but here's a quick example to help you get started. If you like coffee in the morning, what does it feel like to sit in silence truly enjoying its taste while reading a book that inspires you so that by the time your family wakes up, you are in such a good place to help them start their day? No one feels rushed. It's peaceful and calm. Your breakfast is enjoyable, and you have great conversations so that once everyone is on their way to start their day, they are eager for it to begin.

Here's what I discovered. You can have that day. You have the power within you to create it and to make every day special. You know how I know this? Because you are already creating yours. Sit in that thought for a minute. There really is no one dictating to you what your day should be like. You just got into the habit of it and have concluded that there is no way out. Do you want to go through the next decade or two feeling out of control? Or do you want to go to bed at night knowing that you created the best day you could and restful peaceful sleep would come quickly?

When I first became aware that I was in control and was already creating each day, I was blown away that I had the ability to change it, that I could go through the day worried about things that more than likely would never happen or I could set the pace of the day by my choices. I could change my day by changing my mind and my habits. If you will take the time and energy to create your day, then you will create great weeks, great months, and ultimately, remarkable years. You have the power to build the life you dream of, and it is time to step into that power so that you can create that rich girl life.

When you decide to build that day and life that you and your family deserve, you are going to come up against resistance, not only within yourself but with those around you especially when you decide that the network marketing industry is going to help you achieve the life that you are after. There will be people who will tell you it's a scam, that you won't make any real money. Not everyone will support your new goals, simply because they don't have the dream that you have, and once we start to make changes, people sometimes are scared that you might leave them behind or change so much that they won't know you anymore.

Even when you surround yourself with people who are working with you toward those goals, you are going to find that you are your own worst enemy, and I call that your very own poor girl, aka your inner bully, which we will discuss in more detail in the next chapter. This inner bully kicks in big-time and gives you all kinds of reasons that you will fail simply because it loves staying the same and gets really concerned when we are serious about making changes.

We will ask ourselves these question many times, "Can I truly have what I want without it consuming every aspect of my life? Will I get out of balance? What will I need to give up in order to have this day?" These are great questions and will come up often, and there are going to be days where life will take over, and it will seem as if we don't have control, but we do because we can choose how we react to these situations. I have discovered that the way I react to the circumstances of the day helps me to make better decisions and I can base those decisions on what I want instead of reacting and perhaps receiving what I don't want. I will give you an example. You have a full day planned and one of your children gets sick so you start to get upset that your day will not go as planned, however you have a choice here to remain neutral and know that everything is okay, that the most important thing is to take care of your child and that your business can wait. You therefore are calm and caring and not upset, which will cause your day to be less stressful. We talk a lot about balance; however, I haven't found balance to be attainable, because everything is always in flux, so the thought of balance is self-defeating. Women are especially hard on themselves about this elusive balance. We want to have it all, and we work hard at balancing it all but end up frazzled. I stopped trying to balance life, and instead I get into the flow of life. I love this quote from Florence Shinn, "Let God juggle your situations, for when you try to juggle them, you drop all the balls."

I see this happening with a lot of women in the network marketing industry because they are too excited about it. Many have been home for a long time yearning for something, and they feel that they've been missing out on being in the workplace and having adult interactions. So they get into network marketing. Then they want to spend all their time on it because they love the excitement, friendships, and the possibilities of unlimited income along with the recognition. It's great to fall in love with your work, but if you get to a point where you're not taking care of yourself or you're not being present for your family, then something's got to give. Otherwise, you're going to burn out. It can cause problems in marriages, problems with kids, or poor self-care.

One of the biggest fights that Dave and I had when I first started building a business was that I was always on the phone. At first, I denied it. I argued with him about not being on the phone all the time; however, we both knew that was just not true. He blew up early one morning when I received a call from one of my team members. She called while we were having breakfast, and I was in an animated conversation with her. When I looked over at the table, Dave had steam coming out of his ears. He was furious that I took time away from our conversation to pick up the phone even though he did it countless times with his customers, so I had no clue as to why he could be mad. I hung up quickly as he beat both of his hands down on the kitchen table while screaming, "You just don't care about us anymore!" I mean, I was dumbfounded. How could I not care about him or the kids anymore when the reason I was doing the business was for our family? I was on fire for what I was doing. I loved it, and he knew it, and for some reason that made him mad. He believed that I no longer cared as much about the family as I did about the business because I was so darn excited all the time. I was on fire for what I had discovered, and I put my heart and soul into it. I am sure he hadn't seen that kind of excitement coming out of me since our honeymoon—bless his heart. In all serious-ness, I knew that I needed to establish some guidelines, so I instilled a schedule into my business and told my team when I was open for business. That was one of the smartest things I did in the beginning—no more early-morning or late-night phone calls, and honestly my team loved it because they knew they could instill those guidelines into their business and keep their families happy. Many times, you must realize that you need to put the phone down and be present with your family.

Give yourself permission to love the business. Also give yourself permission to take excellent care of yourself and your family. This is *your* responsibility, not the company's, not your mentor's, not anyone else's. In ten years, you want your relationship with your spouse, children, and friends to be healthy. And, your idea of your dream day is going to change over time. Children grow up, you'll get older, your priorities may shift. You have the power to create different dream days for different times in your life.

You are an entrepreneur in network marketing. You are building a business. This doesn't happen in a week, a month, or even a year. It takes time. It's crucial that you pace yourself and take care of yourself. It's important to know that you don't have to do it in a single day or even in a year. The amount of time you can put into your business will determine how fast it grows, but don't make the mistake of doing nothing but your business or make the mistake of doing nothing in your business! I have seen what an extra $500 a month can do for some people, and it's profound. It might mean the difference between worrying about diapers, gas, or not having to count every penny at the grocery store. Your life may be significantly affected in a positive way with an extra $500.

It is also good to define what wealth means to you. This is an important question. It's all about perspective. If I told someone who was living in lack that they could make six figures working from home, they would not believe me. If you are holding yourself to a standard that is created by someone else's perspective or even your own, then you are bullying yourself. I've seen too many people create dream boards based on something that's not realistic for them along with not believing that achieving those dreams will happen for them. Therefore, if you truly don't believe that it will happen for you, then you will not do the things that will take you there. Only when you craft *your* day around *your* why and *your* personal definition of wealth will you begin to see success in this business. Also, note that you are not going to master the rest of your life in one day. Just relax. Master each day. Then just keep doing that *every* day.

ASK YOURSELF:

What does a dream day look like for you?

What are the thoughts in your head that are holding you back?

What do you feel are some of the steps that you will need to take in order to have this day?

Are you ready to make these changes?

Chapter 4

The Poor Girl,
aka Inner Bully

"You don't have to believe everything you say to yourself."
—AUTHOR UNKNOWN

I have found if we want success in our life, it requires us to re-frame how we think and talk to ourselves. In chapter 3 I brief-ly referenced self-bullying. In this chapter I'm going to ask you to confront your poor girl mentality, aka your inner bully. It might be challenging because your inner bully has been with you your entire life, but with persistence and gentleness to-ward yourself, you can become aware of the bully and make her or him your ally or at least come to it with understanding and appreciation. I am going to ask you to do an exercise in this chapter that might be challenging. I'm going to ask you to journal what your inner bully says.

Just the other day Dave and I were walking downtown, and I observed a woman talking to herself out loud and what she was saying was anything but kind. She was scolding herself about a myriad of things. I looked at Dave and said that the saddest part about witnessing this is that we all do this to ourselves all day every day. We do not say it out loud because we don't want to get locked up, but we do have a conversation going, such as, "I'm not smart enough. I'm not good enough. My hair looks awful today." This bully can be mean and nasty. Its mission in life is to keep you where you are so that it feels safe. It will win unless you become aware of it. I have asked people if they talk to themselves, and some look at me as if I am crazy, and then I point out that right now this very second they are doing just that.

I did something that was instrumental in discovering where my mind was at in a pivotal point in my life—a point where I knew things had to change. I needed to grow beyond my current circumstances. I challenged myself to write down over a 48-hour period everything that my inner bully said from the moment I opened my eyes in the morning until I closed them at night and even during the night if I woke. I always kept my journal by my side so I would be ready. Here's a couple of examples. Let's say you make a mistake and get the dates mixed up for an event at your child's school. What does your inner bully say about that? Does it tell you you're disorganized? Does it berate you for making a mistake? Does it say, "You are a bad mom?" How long does it talk? Write down exactly what it says.

You must get quiet with this exercise and take it very seriously. It's not enough to simply notice what your inner bully says to you. You must physically write it down for 48 hours. I want you to understand the impact of these beliefs. Not only are you being unfair to yourself, but you are transferring these patterns and beliefs to your children, family, friendships, and your business. They are the beliefs and thoughts of the poor girl. Once you understand this and see what you are thinking, your eyes will be open, and you can begin to clean up your relationship with yourself. What you must understand is that we all have this inner bully talking trash to us. Sometimes it is in different voices such as the voice of a parent, boss, former teacher, minister, peer, or you as a child. Once you can gain some control over your inner bully by awareness, it will improve how you approach everyone and everything around you!

When you are writing, you must let it flow—no censoring allowed. Don't stop and think, "I wonder what I should write down." As the writing flows, tears and emotions may flow too. There's no right or wrong in this. The idea is simply to identify what your inner bully is saying. Write down as much as you can over the 48-hour period, and then carve out the time that will be necessary for you to read it and be able to ask yourself, "How would I feel if someone else spoke to me like this? Would I speak to a friend or a loved one this way?" I'm betting that you would not allow anyone to talk to you the way you to talk to yourself, or would you speak to anyone in the way you speak to yourself. Look at each thing you wrote down and ask yourself, "Is this really true about me?" Make notes on what you are saying as you read it.

What I discovered is that when my inner dialogue is saying something nasty to me and is making me feel bad about myself, then it's more than likely not true about me because it is making me feel bad about myself; however, in the beginning of my journey into self-awareness, I didn't realize that. I believed that voice, and it could take me down a deep, dark rabbit hole. And almost always it is not even our own voice: it can be a parental voice, a teacher, a peer, the voice of someone in our past, or even, our current life. By completing this exercise, you can start to clear up what your inner bully is saying. You will also become aware that it's likely that your inner bully has been in charge for a very long time.

You're not going to clear out the junk in two days. You must be patient and persistent. Just let the days unfold, always be aware of your thoughts and check to see if they are from your inner bully. Don't fight it; when we fight it, we give it power. Allow the negative thoughts to come in, recognize them for what they are (the bully!), and then let them go on their way. I think of my inner bully's statements as if they are in a cloud, and the cloud just drifts away in the wind. The voice of your inner bully or your inner critic (or whatever you choose to name it) wants to keep you in a box. In that box it feels safe, and when you start to hit on the walls of that box, your inner bully will really start acting up. Once you make up your mind to deal with it and try something new, that critical voice will try to get your attention and squash your new goals. And for me, it was winning in many areas of my life until I started to pay attention and made the decision to change those thoughts.

I haven't perfected quieting the inner bully, but I am aware of it. For example, when I started thinking about writing this book, it said, "You don't have time for that, Pam, there's no way. And what are you going to do, sit there and write all day, you can't do that; you won't have a business left if you devote time to this. How are you going to do that?" It's such a strong voice, and it wants to keep us in our comfort zone. I am constantly practicing dealing with my inner bully, just like you. How did I handle it? I told myself, "Absolutely, I can write this book, and I am going to have fun doing it." That negative voice is strong and powerful; however, you are too. I wouldn't let it win, so I started. I worked on this book day by day, and now you are reading it.

You're going to be okay! Know that there's nothing wrong with you, and you're going to be fine. It just comes down to being clear, aware, and persistent. You are the one giving your power away, defeating yourself, and saying no. You can take your power back from that inner bully just by being aware. Does this mean everything is going to be easy? Of course not! But it can be fun once you understand and decide to pay attention. The decision is yours. Remember, sometimes your thoughts are simply not true. You don't have to believe everything you say to yourself.

As I was building my first business in the industry, I came to understand with a lot of work that I was the cause of my problems. At first, I would look outside and blame it on my upline (the person who recruited me into the company), the company, or my team. However, after doing this exercise multiple times throughout these last two decades, I realize that I am the cause. It is my thinking, and that is powerful because we can change. However, if we get discouraged, then we allow those thoughts to consume us. We give them so much belief and power that you can fall asleep for years in a thought such as, "I'm not good enough." I also understood that these thoughts and beliefs were creating what was happening in my life because they affected the actions that I took. If you don't believe you are good enough, you send out an advertisement to the world, "Look at me, I'm not good enough for this." The world can feel this coming from you, so why would they want to join you in your business? I love this analogy of advertising to the world what we are thinking and feeling. It brings everything into perspective. If you are advertising (thinking, believing) that your team stinks, then you are putting that out there, and why would anyone want to join a team that stinks? If you are advertising that you cannot recruit anybody or that no one wants your product, then guess what: that advertising will bring you back more of that.

Think about the times that you have gone somewhere knowing that you looked amazing and you felt on top of your game; in other words, you felt powerful and in control. The energy bouncing off you caused heads to turn. Both men and women could sense your power, and they wanted whatever you had. I once read an article on Marilyn Monroe. She would walk down Hollywood Boulevard with a friend as Norma Jean Mortenson, which was her real name, and no one would recognize her. Her friend would say, "Turn on Marilyn," so she would immediately change her energy or as we know it today, her state, and transform herself without a change of clothes (no cape, not even a mask) into Marilyn—right on the spot. People would suddenly swarm her, and all she did was become Marilyn who was the rich girl of her beliefs. You can do this too, and you have done it on many occasions. Change your state, and your life will change.

In Michael Singer's book *The Untethered Soul* he states, "True personal growth is about transcending the part of you that is not okay and needs protection. This is done by constantly remembering that you are the one inside that notices the voice talking. That is the way. The one inside who is aware that you are always talking to yourself about yourself is always silent."

Lastly, I have also discovered that this inner bully guides me into knowing what I am afraid of and what my beliefs are about myself. It is good at giving me a mirror into my thoughts about myself, so it can be an ally in life if we allow ourselves the ability to look at these thoughts or beliefs with the right mental attitude. When something pops up and I can step back and look at the thought from an observer's perspective, I can see that I really think that about myself or that thing that keeps showing up in my life, and I no longer want it I have the ability to change it by understanding that it is just a belief that I keep thinking. This can be powerful, so my inner bully can become an inner friend that shows me where I am in life. I love looking at it from this perspective, and I hope that you can also come to terms with this voice.

ASK YOURSELF:

What does your inner bully say to you?

What surprised you about this exercise?

How can you take your power back?

What can you do to take one step toward the life that you want?

Chapter 5

Building Your Dream Day

*"Once you know that you know that you know
what you truly want, then the fire is lit in
your heart and there is no stopping you."*
—PAM SOWDER

The only reason that I was open to looking at an opportunity was because we were going through a transition in our family and Dave, being the practical one in the family, realized the kids were getting to the age where they were involved in several activities, and those activities cost money. He was also thinking about their future: cars, car insurance, college. He was thinking logically, of course, but I was thinking emotionally and visualizing my dream life of being that rich girl who could have it all. And the all was not only the material side of wealth of being able to afford their after-school activities but the family style of wealth, which meant being able to get them ready for school without being rushed and continuing to be there for them when they got off the bus in the afternoon. We had our routines down, and we loved where we were at. So I started looking for jobs that were spare time and part-time.

First, I went back to my goal-setting days when I was selling IBM computers in the early 80s. Through their sales training I learned to set goals and plan out the year. So, each year, I would ask myself, "How are you going to end your year, how are you going to end your month, and how are you going to end your week?" That would determine how I spent my day. Why is it so important to focus on the day and not the end of the year? Let's say that you reach your year's end goal; however, you practically killed yourself getting there, and your family never saw you. Is the goal worth that? I knew it wasn't for me, and I knew from prior experience that if I got up every day and lived for the day while truly enjoying it, then the year would end up being where I wanted it while still having my life intact. It may look like you are winning in your paycheck, but if your days are not fulfilling, then once again, why do it? This was an important lesson that came back to me when I started thinking about going back to work in 1994.

As you start asking for something else or for more, ideas and things come to you, and I've learned to take some of those ideas and go with them but quickly get out if they are not enjoyable or fulfilling. One of my first ideas was to sign up for substitute teaching. Within days I received a call and I was assigned to teach an eighth-grade music class, and boy, was I in for a day because I didn't know a thing about eighth graders, much less music! I felt like my head might explode. It was anything but enjoyable, and it certainly wasn't worth the $50 that I got paid. After class that day, I walked down to the administrative office and asked them to take me off the list. After the substitute teaching fiasco, I helped some of my girlfriends with projects that were crafty in nature; however, I realized very quickly that I needed to pursue things that didn't involve those types of skills. Crafty is not one of my things!

That's when I knew that I needed to create in my mind the type of day that I wanted, not what anyone else wanted for me. As I stated earlier, I had learned this not only through my prior sales training but also the self-development books that I had been reading. Here's the starting foundation of what I first visualized.

As the morning began, I wanted to get the kids off to school without rushing. I knew what it felt like to be rushed in the morning. I worked for three years when our son Adam was born and always felt like the mornings were lost in getting ready, and I knew it would be even more so with two children that needed to be out the door at the same time. Currently, I could spend time with them and ease them into the day with breakfast, pack their lunches, and walk them up to the school bus. After they left, I wanted to have the time to drink a great cup of coffee while reading or listening to something inspirational, get a great workout in, and then get the house in order. I knew that if I didn't take the time for this in the morning, then it probably wouldn't happen. For the fun stuff, how about lunch with the girls or a mani/pedi? We all need and want time for those things. Catching up with friends is an all-time favorite of mine. I get a lot of inspiration from my friends, not to mention how it can be lonely at times while being at home. I think we all love and need those friendships. Doesn't this look like a great way to kick off each morning all the way through lunch and the afternoon?

Once the kids got off the bus, I wanted to be able to spend some quality time with them, because I noticed that they always wanted to tell me things. If I didn't catch them right away, then those thoughts would get lost, and I didn't want to miss out on that. After that, I helped them dive into their homework, made them a good dinner, and could be there for bath and bedtime. Oh, and do not forget, Big Daddy needed some time too. That would be a dream day for us, and I wondered if, in between all of that, there was anything I could do in the nooks and crannies of that day.

In all seriousness, this was what I clearly visualized; however, I was willing to see the girlfriends less and get my morning routine down to a science. In other words, let's get real.

As Dave was saying the job word, and I was crafting my dream day, I didn't see how they could go together. Dave did a lot of entertaining with his job, and we always had amazing dinners with his customers. One night as we headed out for a two-hour drive to take his most valued customer out to dinner, I spoke to him about how I wanted my day to play out, and of course, he didn't get how that could possibly work, so that idea was pretty much lost on him. At that dinner, I spoke about it again and told the couple we were having dinner with that I was looking for something to do and that I had crafted out a dream day and what that would look like and in between all the things I wanted to find something to do. We all had a good laugh, except deep inside, this is what I wanted.

Several weeks went by while I was scouring the newspaper and asking friends if they knew of anything that could possibly work for me when the customer that we had taken out to dinner called me up on a Monday and invited me to that first meeting. He said he thought he'd found an answer to creating my dream day. I asked him what he meant and what it was. He wouldn't tell me much of anything, only that I should go and listen. He said he'd attended a meeting several days before and liked what he heard, so he joined the company and he thought I might want to join it too. That is when all the red flags went up. What did he mean by join, and what went on at this meeting? I didn't badger him too much, because after all he was Dave's customer, so I told him I would go without any intention of going, just so I could get him off the phone. I thought I was being nice and it would all go away after that night, but I was wrong. He called me the following Wednesday morning and asked me what I thought of the meeting. I made something up about not going, and he said, "That's okay because they will be there the following Tuesday and the Tuesday after that, so I'll keep calling until you go!" Oh my gosh, I was going to have to go. As you read earlier, that meeting was a turning point in our lives. It was exactly what I had been asking for to complete my dream day.

As the months and years went by, that dream day started to unfold, and I did create this day by utilizing the vehicle of network marketing, and you can too. It didn't happen immediately. It took time. Network marketing is an industry where you can work within the parameters like the ones I had and build an income that for most people seems impossible. As I stated earlier, all I was looking for in the beginning was $1,000 a month, but as my confidence and belief level grew, I saw that there could be much more.

Even twenty-five years later I still feel like I'm living that dream day. Some things have changed, but I still start my morning with inspiration and a great cup of coffee while getting my workout in. Starting my business in the early days with this dream day in mind along with my why is what has kept me going and not giving up, and that is why I teach this to everyone.

Would you like to create your dream day? I know that it will be powerful for you to take the time to do this, so let's start. Be very clear about what you want from the moment you open your eyes in the morning. What would make you want to jump out of bed, eager to start the day? What happens each hour throughout the day? How will the entire day play out? Write it out by hand. Get the nicest paper or journal you can find, and luxuriate in the experience of writing it out. If you're having a conversation with someone, what are you playing out? Throughout that entire day, are the kids happy? Are they living great lives? How's business? Is it exploding? Do you have meetings planned? Are you training a team? Are you meeting new people? Write it all out, and keep going back to it. Make it vivid so it's like the movie of your life, and you are not only the actor but the director and producer.

Try to resist the urge to cram as many things as you can into your day. I don't want you to sacrifice the things that are important to you in order to drive your success. I truly believe you can have it all, but what does that really mean? It's different for everyone. Some of us have one child, some have four. Some are married, some are single. One of the things I've noticed is that people tend to argue for their limitations. For example, "I'm a single mom, my husband's not onboard, my friends are making fun of me, and so forth." We look at these things as limitations. I would like to suggest that you use them as inspiration instead. Let what you think are limitations inspire you and drive whatever is hungry in you.

Now start to live in this day as though your business is already built. This is what I did, and for me it meant getting up earlier so that I could have that leisurely cup of coffee while reading something inspirational. It meant being more organized with the morning preparations to get the kids off to school. It meant having non-negotiables such as going to the gym and taking care of the house. It also meant a non-negotiable time for working my business. I knew I needed to come from a place of being professional, which meant being consistent in my daily activities that got me paid, which is bringing in customers and distributors. I could not afford to waste time or energy. I had to put in the daily work.

There will be moments when things don't go according to your dream day, and that's normal, but I found that I had to give that life situation the time that it needed, but I also had to get right back into that day so that it wouldn't throw me off for weeks. Life happens to all of us; however, it doesn't have to take us out of the game. Reevaluate when you need to, let the negative stuff go, and jump right back into your dream day.

Everything I am asking you to do is because I have lived it and experienced it. I have gained much wisdom since my early days in network marketing about overcoming limitations and dealing with my internal bully. I see it all the time—people who want something really badly, but they can't get out of their own way because they are constantly bullying themselves or allowing someone else to. It's unbelievable that we do this to ourselves and that we can live this way for decades without even knowing that we are doing it. This much I know is true—if you keep playing the same thoughts over and over in your mind, you won't be successful in creating the day that you want. Life will stay the same.

I wish that I knew back in those very early days what I know now, because I lived in such fear—fear of the unknown, fear of what people would think, fear of not being good enough, fear of being laughed at, fear of not having the knowledge, fear of not being able to answer the questions. I learned that these fears were just habits or belief systems that I either overheard as a child or picked up along the way from well-intentioned people. It has nothing to do with not having a good upbringing or good parents. It happens to all of us.

As you become more familiar with your poor girl mentality or inner bully, you can begin to recognize these patterns of thoughts and catch them early enough within the day, or before you know it your entire day reflects those very thoughts. That is why it is so important to start your day with daily inspiration because life will bring you things throughout the day; however, if you start off with the right mental attitude, then you can handle them better, and you will find that you don't spiral down that rabbit hole of negativity.

In this chapter, I've asked you to write a lot of things down. I want you to really dive deep into developing your vision for your dream day, living from your dream day, noticing what your inner bully is saying, and countering that bully with positive thoughts and ideas of knowing that you can accomplish what you want. I want you to come back to this chapter frequently and reevaluate and hone your vision. This process is worth the time that it takes for you to create it, and it's going to be ongoing for the rest of your life. Like anything in life, if you practice daily, you will get better and better. These practices combined with knowing your why will turn your mindset around, and you will find that there is nothing you can't do.

Lastly, throughout my day I am always listening to powerful wisdom whether that is via a podcast, YouTube, Audible, and so forth. In the early days, I would burn out cassette tapes listening in my car. My children could mouth the words of Jim Rohn, Tony Robbins, Earl Nightingale, and many others. I knew that the bully could take over if I didn't feed my mind daily. It is just as important as feeding your body. I also exercised daily. It's a must. Studies now show that when the body moves, the brain moves. That is why on walks I get such great ideas. Fall in love with these two very beneficial and important non-negotiables. Make the time, and then time will give you what you want.

ASK YOURSELF:

Are you ready to live your best day every day?

What would your day be like if you could create it just the way you want it?

What are your non-negotiables each day?

What do you feel is stopping you?

Chapter 6

Your Money Mindset

"Poverty is but the sleep of wealth."
—Neville Goodard

What is your money mindset? Your money mindset is your beliefs and attitudes about money. It is what you feel you are worth. Do you think like a rich girl or a poor girl? Want to find out quickly what your beliefs are around money? Go look at your current situation around money. What is the average amount of money in your checking account each month? In your savings account? Are you in debt? Are you stuck at a certain amount each month? Do you worry about money? Does it keep you up at night? Do you argue over it? Do you feel unworthy when it comes to making money?

If you want to make it big as far as money goes in network marketing or life in general, you must develop a strong sense of self-worth, and that begins with becoming aware of your money mindset and what money means to you. If you want to feel good about money, it must be about more than just writing checks to good causes.

The subject of money causes us to go silent because we are taught not to talk about it. I can trace my first thoughts about money back to my childhood. I am fortunate that my parents instilled some great core values in me about money, such as don't waste it, don't overspend it, don't use credit cards, budget, and some not so good ones, such as, money doesn't grow on trees, the rich get richer, who do you think you are for wanting more, and so forth—not to mention the other adults in my life who were also freely giving me their money mindsets and had lived through the depression or the worst of times.

My parents tried to give us everything in life that they possibly could, and I don't remember wanting for anything, but there was an underlying sense of there not being enough money at times. I also saw a side of money that I didn't like, and that was fighting about it. I experienced heated arguments between my parents around money, and I knew that at whatever cost I wanted to avoid that in my life. Seeing this instilled a sense of lack and fear in me that I have had to work on multiple times throughout in my life.

It's important to examine your beliefs about money as we redefine what wealth means to us. What was your first perception of money? What is your earliest money memory? For me, I remember I found a quarter in a mud puddle when I was four or five. My mother asked me if she could have it. At that time, there just wasn't much money in my family. My dad worked two jobs, and there was myself, my older sister, and younger brother. My mom was a stay-at-home mom once my sister was born, so she had not personally earned money for many years. She valued that quarter, and I knew that it meant a lot to her, but I also knew within me that it was just a quarter. I didn't like it that she needed it, and that made me sad because like most children, I wanted much, much more for my mother. This one moment had such a profound effect on me that I remember it to this day and think what it must have been like for my mother, who didn't have the same opportunities as me or take the risks that I was willing to take. I knew I had to win, and from a very early age I decided that I would work hard and never have to worry about money. I would become that rich girl.

I also remember my parents sitting down every month to pay the bills. My mom had great handwriting, so she would write the checks. My dad kept the list of what was owed and who it was owed to. About the time they got halfway down the list, the anger would set in, and dad would begin to question what she spent the money on if those bills were hers. As I look back, I believe he was feeling inadequate. He was doing everything he could, but it was never enough. I promised myself that I would never live like that. I didn't want to argue over money or have my children watch their parents arguing each month.

My parents are still alive today, and they have one of the best marriages I've ever seen, and that is because they have a deep caring love for each other. So those times that I remember them getting upset over money had a profound effect on me. I saw that if not having enough money could be one of the reasons parents fight, then having enough could be the cause for a happier marriage. I didn't want to fight over something like money, and I didn't expect it to come easy. I knew I would "get to" earn it, and I was willing to do just that.

Discovering the industry of network marketing showed me exactly where my money mindset was: the exact amount at each phase of my life. The first time is when I set my goal of earning $1,000 per month. I got there in the fourth month that I started working my business. The next month it stayed right at $1,000—again, my goal. My sponsor called that month as he always did and asked me what my check was, and when I told him, he said, "You made that last month. Why didn't you double it?" I was speechless. It never dawned on me to make more. I hit my goal of $1,000. Why would I want more? Then he said something that shook me out of my complacency. He said, "You have already proven that you can more than double your check, so why not keep on doing that?" I woke up. I was going to stay at the $1,000 a month if I didn't set a new goal or belief for myself. So I doubled it and continued to do that for months, and then I got stuck again. I needed to dive even deeper into why I wanted more and get past my limiting beliefs of what I thought I was worth. It has been one of my deepest works, and it starts with taking a strong look at where you are at and if that is where you want to be. It is asking the bigger question of, "Why am I here, and what is causing me to feel that this is what I am worth, or why am I feeling guilty for wanting more?" Then I get silent and allow the answers to come. It might take a day or a few weeks; however, I always get my answer, and it typically blows me away. It's a belief that I keep thinking; therefore, it keeps me where I am at and nothing grows. It's the worst form of stuck.

Here is another story of someone I have worked with who was stuck at earning $3000 a month in her network marketing business. No matter what she did, she could not get beyond that $3,000. I asked her what she did before she started her direct sales career, and she responded that she had been a teacher. When I asked her what her salary was as a teacher, she responded that she had earned $36K a year. Guess what? That breaks down to $3,000 a month! She believed that $3,000 a month was all that she was worthy of, so that is what she got to and stayed stuck at. Her money mindset was based at $3,000 per month, and anything beyond was too unfamiliar.

Have you ever heard that something like 70 percent of all lottery winners are broke within a couple of years after they win the lottery? Why does that happen? It's because they are used to making less than $50,000 a year and then suddenly find themselves with millions, and they don't know how to manage it or how to act. They unconsciously do whatever they can to get rid of the money! Their money mindset does not match their newly acquired income and is too unfamiliar. See, most people do not have a problem with money, they have a problem with scarcity. They feel that they aren't good enough or they don't deserve to have everything they want. So our problems with money will almost never be solved with more money. Think about it. You make more money, and then you blow it. You get out of debt and get right back into debt. You achieve a higher rank in your business with more money only to stop doing the things that you did to get there, so your check goes down. It's not that you don't know what to do, you simply stopped doing it because you have a scarcity mentality. You might be thinking, "Everything I have, I eventually lose. Nothing lasts forever." I've seen it happen too many times. Money mindset, like your success mindset, is an inside job. And, it can work both ways: poor girl to rich girl or rich girl to poor girl.

You must look at yourself and be open and honest if you are stuck with your money mindset. You must ask yourself these questions: Why do I feel like this? Where is this money belief coming from? Why do I feel that this is all I am worth? It is deep inner work. If you can become aware of your beliefs around money, you put yourself in a position to learn new beliefs. Everyone is worthy of making whatever money they want to make. There is no shortage of abundance. It's everywhere if you open your mind and your eyes to it.

You can also reframe it by thinking about money in an entirely new way, and this is what worked for me. I was not raised that I could be a rich girl; however, I knew deep down inside that that was what I wanted, so I needed to change my poor girl mentality around money. I started looking at money as energy and a form of service. See, if you make a new relationship with something, you can shed your old beliefs and make a new familiar one. This allowed me to give and receive money more easily. Money, as everything else, doesn't want to remain stagnant. It likes to flow, and that is what is meant by cash flow.

When I first got started in the industry and before I was making "bank" I knew that I needed to not feel poor anymore. I knew that feeling poor was a low source of energy, and no one wanted to be around poor energy, and I certainly didn't want more of that scarcity mentality in my life. All poor does is bring on poorer. Think about low energy and the times when you were in debt and how low you felt. You had no energy. You didn't feel good, and you certainly didn't want to do anything. You sat around, and you sulked. Start noticing these feelings, and when you are with people and they start down the path of talking about what they don't have, notice their body language as well as their words. You will hear things such as, "Why does this always happen to me?" "I can't get anyone to join my team." "No one wants to be my customer." "Money is so hard to come by."

Can we build the skills to look at money differently? I know we can because once I understood this, I started watching how I acted and what I thought. I also asked, "What do we naturally do in this business as a way of increasing our checks?" We perform acts of service in the form of recruiting distributors, gathering customers, training, and leadership. These are the services that we perform daily. So if money can be a direct reflection of the services that I perform, then I want to perform them at 100 percent. The more service and the form of service in the way of being great that I put out there, the more that came back in the way of service and money. The less service I put out there, the less that came back in the way of service and money. Money flows as I flow.

I started writing down my beliefs about money and reframing those beliefs such as "I can never make enough money" to "Money flows easily to me." From, "No one wants to be in my business" to "Everyone wants to be in my business because we offer the best training and leadership." Once again, great acts of service.

Let's go back to the former teacher frustrated that she was only earning $3,000 per month. She was self-sabotaging. Once we had a conversation and she became aware of what was going on, she went from $3,000 to $30,000 a few months later. That's just from becoming aware and understanding and trusting that there is always going to be enough. Now, most of us ask, "How did she do that? Did she work harder? Did she get a windfall of people?" and so forth. What happened was her inner belief shifted that she and her family were worth more, and therefore they were worthy of the increase, so she allowed her beliefs to shift, and the people showed up and joined her team, and her check increased.

Once we allow our thoughts and dreams to come in along with feeling that they are happening, the how shows up along with the people, places, and things that we need. Her actions were based on her newfound belief of more than $3,000 per month. She stepped into the thought of "more." Again, you don't need to know how you are going to get there, but you need to know that you are worth it and where you want to go.

Have you ever heard the saying "Like attracts like?" As you are building a network marketing team, look at the people around you. Are they doers or do they just stand by and wait for someone to tell them what to do or wait for someone to do it for them? Do they jump in the game and start working? Are they team players? When you begin to work on your money mindset you will attract people to your team who have the same mindset, so early on I made a list of the attributes of the people I wanted on my team: driven, inspired, fun, connected, action orientated, coachable, and so forth. This list is still being added to today. I have over a hundred attributes of the type of people that I want in my life and on our team. I also realize that I work daily on being everything on that list to attract these people.

I have had multiple experiences with getting stuck and having to work on my money mindset. There were so many times when I would get to a certain rank or check and stay there or lose the rank and thousands of dollars. Before I understood that it was my very own self-limiting beliefs that held me back, I would blame my team, the products, the company, the lack of support, the comp plan, and so forth. It is way easier to look outside of ourselves and start blaming others and things that seem out of our control. However, that never worked. I could get a new product or a new team that would start some momentum only to fall back again. What the heck was going on? I got to the point where I couldn't blame anyone else because others were achieving what I wanted, so I knew it had to be me. Ouch! However, I also felt empowered because if it was me, then I could work on me and not have to control everything and everyone else.

I realized that I wanted it so badly that I was living in the lack of it. I was living in what was not working, who was not working, all those outside things and people that weren't doing what I needed them to do so I could get rich. I also knew that no matter where I went, I would take me with me, so I had to take a long look at who I was, so I reached out for help by asking God to show me. Show me what I need to do, and I'll do it. He has a strange way of showing us things. We think it is going to be something it never is, and mine came in the way of a five-day workshop in New York that shook me to the core both mentally and physically. I came out of there knowing that it is an inside job, that my money mindset was focused on lack—the poor girl mindset—that I had to walk in the belief and know that it was happening whether I could at the present see it or touch it, so I decided that I was going to focus on the day. I came out knowing that I was going to walk into each day happy and fulfilled, that life is too short to keep trying to change the ending. We need to change the beginning, so I knew that each day it was important to wake up and truly live in the moment of that day. With even more conviction, I stepped into the day that I had created in my mind. I woke up earlier. I drank my coffee and read something that got my mind right. I exercised and fed my body what it needed. I got my house in order. I had my work list of what I would accomplish that day, and I never compromised that list. I got it done, and I did it happy with expectancy. Again, happy doesn't come once you are there, happy is something you decide on. I decided that each day was important and that each day was the journey, the adventure, and I was going to live it. I was going to live in abundance and gratitude. And at night I thanked God for my day and the fruits of that day. It started working. I started having fun and the stress left. The abundance came and never left me. I truly know that if I walk in the faith and belief of abundance with happiness and knowing that it is done, then so be it. And you can too. Decide what you are wanting is the first step; then create your day filled with happiness. It really is that simple, and the key is to not get in your own way and to know that you are profoundly worth it.

ASK YOURSELF:

What is my current mindset about money?

What are my feelings when I think about money?

What do I earn on average each month?

What do I dream about earning?

What needs to change to remove the roadblock to my success?

How can I reframe money?

How can I give more acts of service, and what would they look like?

Chapter 7

Ten-Mile Radius

"Don't waste one day wondering what people are thinking."
—PAM SOWDER

Big Daddy (Dave) and I love to watch movies. We were watching a sci-fi movie one night, and one of the characters knew he was about to be killed off, and as he sat there talking to the girl beside of him, he said, "I've never been outside of this town's ten-mile radius. I should have done more. I should have left." Those few sentences had a profound effect on me, and I thought about my life and my hometown and how I grew up, so I wanted to share my thoughts on this throughout this chapter.

If you're like most people, you probably grew up in or near the same town where you live now. Your parents, grandparents, and relatives may have lived close by, which can be really fortunate if you all got along with each other. Think about where you shopped or where your friends lived and where you went to school. Chances are those places were also in a ten-mile radius. That can be a beautiful thing because it can make a child feel very secure and loved. That's how I grew up. My grandparents, uncles, aunts, cousins were all right there. To this day, I still have family and friends, many decades later, who have not moved out of that ten-mile radius. They stay where they are with what they know—very complacent and comfortable. For some, to make a move after many decades in the same place is scary and monumental. And that move is more than a physical move: it can also be a financial move. So few people ever get beyond that, and yet, there's so much more out there; however, I realize it is not for everyone. But what if?

When Dave and I decided to move from our ten-mile radius after living there for five decades, we were both scared and optimistic. We love our family and friends along with the knowingness of where everything was; however, as we got closer to our new state and home, the excitement grew, and we have never looked back. It has opened us up in many ways to growth and longevity, to new friendships and many more opportunities. In the years since, I have realized that we have got to make the move, any move. It can be a new neighborhood, a new job, a new opportunity, a new group of friends, a new style of music, a new style of clothes, a new haircut. A move helps get us out of our complacency.

According to Kris Vallotton's book *Poverty, Riches & Wealth*, "Complacency is to the mind what cancer is to the body. It seeps into the hearts of people and slowly anesthetizes its victims, until finally it chokes the hope out of people."

I don't know about you, but I know I don't want this for my life, so I continually ask for new opportunities, new ways of conducting business, and new people in my life, along with more growth in all areas. When you start asking, you start receiving the inspiration to go somewhere and do something different. Go to workshops and seminars. Join a new club. Do anything to get you out of your routine. Hire a new hair stylist. Join a gym. Make a move.

When you're on your deathbed, do you want to be thinking, "Wow, I'm glad I played it safe and stayed put in one spot. I am glad I didn't take that new job or start that opportunity." When you think about how easy it is to get on a plane or in your car anytime to go anywhere, it's amazing. Not to mention the entrepreneurial opportunities that open daily. People are much more mobile today than they were even ten years ago. Why are we so afraid to leave our ten-mile radius? And this doesn't mean just in distance, this is also in thoughts. This is a question that I would ask and then get very still and listen for the answer. If I had not given network marketing, which seemed like the last thing that I should try a chance, I would not be living the life of abundance that I am currently living. I have always been blessed with God in my life, family, and friends, but the financial stress was there too, and this opportunity has taken that burden away. For that, I will forever be thankful.

Some people seem to get stuck in their high school era because to them that was their pinnacle in life. I see that in business as well. But when someone decides that they're going to be successful, they've got to do something different. It's a conscious decision. Success doesn't come from staying in the same place. Labels follow us when we stay in the same place, and they want to follow us into our new life choices. When you decide you're going to do something great and you're around people who have known you forever—people who know what you drive, what you eat, how many marriages you've had, what your education is, who your family is—they are basing everything on your past and projecting it back on to you. When you make a conscious decision that you don't want that anymore and you gain the courage to make a move, it's easy to get sucked right back into all that negativity, and those former projections can become a self-fulfilling prophecy. You start believing that you are your past and how others have labeled you. It takes strength, but you can make a conscious decision to not listen and not go back. People who have known the "past" you, sometimes don't welcome the change in you because it causes them to look at themselves. They are more comfortable when you stay the same. This can be discouraging and cause you to second-guess your decision. Don't stop dreaming and taking risks. Don't settle into comfortable, which is a slow-death zone.

It would take another book to write down all the labels that I believed about myself and the thoughts that others thought about me. Some of the things that people said or that I heard that they said were heartbreaking. At times, even Dave was disbelieving, and that was the hardest for me to overcome; however, I made up my mind, and we worked through the challenges. I stayed focused and looked past what people said into my future. I knew what I wanted was not in the past. I left that life behind, and I wasn't going back.

It starts with you making a conscious decision and then doing something different. Don't look back waiting for others to come with you. Most won't—at least not for now. They're living in that same state of mind that you were in before that moment, but, believe me, they're watching. If we relate this to network marketing, it usually involves you getting to a certain income for people to really believe in you. Most importantly, this is not for everyone. It may not be their journey, and we need to respect that. I have friends that I hold dearly that are not a part of my business, and that is okay because they give me so many other gifts that help me daily, and I treasure them deeply.

This is critical for you to understand so that you don't give up hope and quit. Network marketing is a unique industry that is evolving and growing. People are starting to pay attention to it and to take it seriously as a career choice. They are looking at it differently than they did even five years ago, because of social media. Social media is changing our industry because people are seeing that working side gigs and building security by having a plan B is valuable and essential in today's economy. It is becoming their plan A and B. We are all becoming influencers on social media, and we can use this platform to build relationships, sell products, and offer our opportunity to work from home. This is changing the way people look at our industry.

I attended a TED talk recently where a judge asked me what I did, and when I told her, she told me those things don't work, which some of you will hear daily, not only in the beginning but decades later. And as I sat there, I could have become defensive or angry; however, I knew that she was coming from a lack of knowledge. Not everyone gets it. So when this happens, don't argue or become defensive. They don't know what you know. What is beautiful about today's world is this industry is social media amplified, which gives us a way to quickly increase wealth while focusing on our own lives, our goals, and our families.

In years past it was frowned upon and was not considered something that anyone would really want to do; however, it was an underground profitable movement. The youth coming of age have less preconceived notions and more curiosity. They know we are social creatures and that purchasing from friends and family is normal today.

People ask; "You mean I talk about these products that I love and use every day and become an influencer to my friends? You mean that you're going to track my success and that of my teams for me, and it's all electronic? You are saying that I can work from my phone anywhere and at any time? You are also saying that I can earn what I want and that there are no ceilings?" Yes, this is what we do and teach.

For some, their friends and family may not understand, but to them it's a natural fit. It's cool to hawk sneakers if you're a pro basketball player. It's an excellent source of income to be a mega star and promote a clothing line. And, it's suddenly cool to do network marketing. It's empowering and fun, and I love it.

Because of social media, the ten-mile radius has expanded and has allowed each one of us to have endless possibilities to build a worldwide business from the comfort of our home. Does that mean you should never leave home? No! When you do, you're going to find a big world out there that is very welcoming and that does care about you. So I say, stretch yourself and get out more! Step up and say, "I'm ready for more." That's the beauty of this business. If millions of people worldwide are buying these products, there must be something to it. It doesn't matter if your resume says high school dropout, stay-at-home mom, millennial, boomer, engineer, teacher, or astronaut.

You can be anything you want to be. You can have anything you want to have.

You can transfer your sales ability and communication skills to this industry, and you don't need sales ability or strong communication skills to earn millions in this industry.

Don't think you can? Just look at the thousands that are. If they can do it, so can you!

You too can go from a poor girl to a rich girl.

When you decide to join a network marketing business and you begin to invest in your personal growth and begin to understand the way the business works and how to duplicate your efforts, you will begin to rank advance. Once you get to a certain income level, your family, friends, and co-workers can't help but notice the change in you. First and foremost, they see confidence in you that they've never seen before. They will see a change in the way you present yourself. After a while you may want to buy a nice new car or move into a different type of home, but we coach people first to get out from underneath suffocating debt and to explore all the options that will help you get the material things you want. Not only will your financial wealth improve, but your physical health will too. You will be giving back to those organizations that you have always wanted to. Most products in this industry are of superior quality, and we're not packing on that middleman (advertising and marketing expenses) that forces many companies to charge much, much more. We are paying you to be the influencer.

Let me make one thing clear. Nobody is "lucky" at this business. Nobody got in at the right time and that's why it soared for them. What they did is create a compelling "why" when they joined, and they went to work on themselves and on their business as if their hair was on fire. That's what it takes. It's an inside job and always has been. On the outside, the playing field is even. This business is such a big mind game. The biggest obstacle that I see happening with almost everyone when looking at it for the first time is excuses. People say things such as, "You're lucky, it was so easy for you" and "If I didn't have four kids, I could do it too." People say things like these because they are living in fear, and their excuses justify their decisions not to try. We create excuses to give us a way out of the conversation.

Life is supposed to be joyful. Why shouldn't your work be? I did okay in my first company, but really, I was mediocre. I look back and know that if I had gotten out of my own way, more results would have happened for me. It was a training ground for me to understand myself and people and to learn the dynamics of the industry and how to build a system within the industry. I was with my first company for over six years, and it gave me the knowledge that I needed along with the confidence to help start our current company. I still had my self-doubts. Could I really lead this many people? Could I really be that owner and that leader that I truly wanted to be? It stressed me out a lot in the beginning because I lacked faith in myself. You're out there, you're building this new company, and you take on full responsibility and feel like it is all on you. If you are as fortunate as I am, you have great partners and co-workers, but ultimately, it's on you because they are doing different jobs and are under different stresses. Of course, all this stress is self-inflicted, but those are mind games we play with ourselves. I went through several years at a high level of stress. Work wasn't fun. At the beginning I thought, "This is going to be a blast," but it wasn't because I realized it wasn't just about building something for myself but that other families and distributors were involved. I felt responsible for everyone, and that took the fun out of it for me until I got over myself.

As I mentioned earlier, I attended a five-day workshop in upstate New York. It was a millionaire mindset intensive called "Warrior Camp." I did things with my body during those five days that I never thought possible. I did things with my mind that I never thought possible. On the last day we walked on thirty-five feet of hot coals. Think about how long that is—of hot coals! I could not have done that on day one. But by day five, it was like I never touched those coals. I was so confident. I worked hard on giving up all those past beliefs about myself and truly discovered that they were no longer who I was or wanted to be.

I came home with the realization that what I was doing was not about the end goal but about the everyday life. I realized it's about living life daily and being present. Whoever is in front of you is who you are supposed to be present with. At that time, I was raising my children, and I wasn't present for them or my husband. That's what was causing most of my stress. And then when I was out on the road, I was not present there either because my mind was still back at home feeling guilty for leaving the kids. Because I was feeling guilty all the time, nothing was fun. Being present is where the fun is! That means being fully "on" wherever you are and giving your all in that moment without worrying about the next day or the next five years—just being fully engaged in your day. That doesn't mean you don't plan. You must plan and put things in your calendar, or they will never happen. But where you are now is where you must be present. So when you are with your children, be fully present by putting the phone away and engage with them. Talk to them. Look them in the eye. Do not try to be multitasking with your phone when you are with them. The magical thing I discovered is that when I gave them solid, undivided attention, ten or fifteen minutes would go by, and they were done with me and ready to go do something on their own. The important thing was that they got their mommy time. That's when I started to enjoy my days again.

Here I am, two and half decades later, and I'm still enjoying every single day. I'm not waiting for the end because there is no end. I'm not waiting to get it done because you never get it done. As soon as you do something, there's something else to do. As soon as you achieve one thing, there's more to achieve. It's called life. Life can bring you hurt and happiness, and it's always changing. So you've got to stay present in the moment and not get derailed. Once I was able to do that, everything changed for me: the way I talked, the way I showed up in the world, the way I live my life. Whether I'm on an airplane or working around the house, I give it my full attention, knowing that the things I might be worried about are probably not going to happen, and I owe it to myself to enjoy each moment. That way when you arrive wherever you're going, you're fully present for the people who need you, and they can tell you care. When you can go through life like that, the wins are great, but the losses don't destroy you because you're present and enjoying every day in a fulfilling way, knowing that those so called losses are there to guide you to the wins.

If you live your life and run your business in a present-day way, you will take people under your wing and teach them how to build a business. You will care about them and train them the right way, working with the ones who really, really want it. There are skills you can learn along the way, and when you get there, there are going to be people with you, cheering you, thanking you, and praying over you. And then you're going to get up every day and you're going to move the people who are with you into their next level, which takes you to your next level. I've watched people do this. I've watched them build both ways—the hard way and the fun and caring way. And when they get to the finish line, they are two different kinds of people entirely. The first is burnt out without a team cheering them on, and the second are happier, more exuberant with a team that is beside of them.

You can be the second type of person. If you can't see yourself as this person right now, then go to work on your mindset. I know people who are approaching retirement, and they can't retire because there's just not enough money. I know moms who want to leave their jobs and come home to be with their children. I know people who can't stand what they are doing but feel there is no way out. They do not wake up happy every day. They wake up stressed. They go through the same routine day after day, not growing, not stretching, having the same conversations, and sharing the same gossip. It serves them in some way because it's comfortable and feels good. But many have not paid attention to their finances. Do you want to be where you were at 35 when you are 70? You've got way more to offer than those who stay in one place. I know you do, and my desire is to help you recognize it and inspire you to change. It's never too late.

ASK YOURSELF:

Do I need to make a move, and if so, what can I do now to get me moving in the direction of my dreams?

Do I allow other's thoughts and actions stop me in achieving my desires?

Am I complacent?

Am I living within my ten-mile radius doing the same things repeatedly?

Chapter 8

What Drives You?

*"You have an untold story within you
and we want to hear it."*
—Pam Sowder

I always knew, even as a kid, that whatever I did in life, it was going to be centered on helping people, and I thought that would be teaching. While I do teach, it's just in a different setting than a classroom. It's in the setting of life. It became my drive and my purpose, because I loved how it made me feel. Helping others was something that came completely natural to me. There is nothing in life that gives me more joy than to see someone start to believe in themselves. To see them step outside of their past and into their present awareness that they are enough.

Having a purpose-filled life, giving, and serving is what I get to do every day, whether it's in business or in everyday life, and I believe that for the rich girl, it is the adult report card of more fulfilling relationships, stronger families, higher paychecks, more friends, more opportunities, freedom of expression, and a huge belief in ourselves. The more we hoard our gifts and talents, the more we stay stuck in the poor girl world, which diminishes our paychecks and soon causes us to stay stuck in every form of lack.

I also discovered in life that if I focused my time and energy on just making money and left out the purpose of helping others, it always left me feeling unfilled and broken in spirit. This happened in the beginning of my career. I was so focused on myself and the rank that I could achieve along with the paycheck that I didn't care how I treated people. I thought of them as a "spot filled." I honestly didn't think of them other than a potential paycheck. I just wanted to make bank and rank, so I pushed and pulled people around. I manipulated them, and at the time I thought I was doing the right thing. I was promoting, and because I pushed and pulled them, they were too; however, I soon discovered a time bomb, and that bomb was about to explode. You see, if you don't respect people and you use them, eventually they will sense this, and everything will blow up. They quit. They become discouraged. They ask you for more. This never works, and it made me and them feel so unworthy. I had lost my purpose. I was acting like a poor girl, who desperately needed to get rich, so I would use and abuse people. You see, people are not "spots"—they are human beings. I had to change and go back to my purpose of helping people, which gave me an even bigger drive of promoting and earning money but in a healthy way, a way where everyone wins.

You can discover what drives you by looking at what you do every day and noticing those moments when you feel good; when you are having those giddy feelings of, "I could do this forever"; when you light up; when you heart feels full; when you could do the work every day and not get paid, but you would feel fulfilled. People used to say to me, "You work all the time." I know I would look back at them dumbfounded because it never felt like work to me. I fell in love with what I was doing.

Many people think in the beginning of their business that they have nothing to offer. They aren't making money yet; they don't have results with the products. All they have is a belief that something might be possible, so how can they find that drive to step out and do the thing? Look, we all felt that way. When I first started, I didn't know if it was going to work, but I believed that it might. I didn't have any results, and people would ask me, "How much are you making?" I soon discovered that if I said, "$15.78" or "fifteen thousand," that it was either too small or too big. So I would turn it around and ask them, "How much would you like to make?" I always turned the question around to them. People are more interested in themselves than in you and what you potentially have to offer them, so always keep their best interests at heart, and turn every question around to them.

You can always be an inspiration for someone through your actions and most importantly through your story. Tell the story of what you found and where you are going. Tell the story of earning $25 and how that helped put gas in your car or bought diapers. Tell the story of dreaming to stay home with your children. No matter how much money you are making, it really comes down to what that money has done for you and what it is going to do for you. This is what moves people.

Stories are how I built my business. Become an incredible storyteller and watch your life change as your stories build.

The other side of drive and purpose is facing fear. I have discovered that there are three aspects of fear: How to handle fear when it comes to stepping into your purpose, how can we use it as a tool or fuel to drive us, and why do we want to bring fear along with us.

So what is fear? You've probably heard the saying that fear stands for "false evidence appearing real." I think that can seem frivolous when people hear it because fear is very real, and you do yourself and others a disservice to discount it. Fear can and does paralyze us. Before I became a distributor for my first network marketing company in 1994, I already had some sales experience. I'd sold IBM computers and had teaching and speaking experience, and I rarely felt fearful unless I really had to do something different; however, I quickly got over it. So for me to experience paralyzing fear the moment that I became a distributor for a network marketing company baffled me. It's like an overwhelming negative presence came over me, and I couldn't do anything. I was afraid to ask people to look at the opportunity. I was terrified to ask my mom, friends, neighbors to become customers. I just shut down. I thought, "What did I sign up for?" I was afraid of the ask and again not being able to answer a question, not being successful, not being able to lead. So I did what they asked me to do in the beginning. I wrote down the names of people who I thought would be a great customer or distributor. My sponsor at the time kept calling me about deadlines that needed to be met so that I could earn what was called the fast start bonus. I didn't meet the deadline because I was paralyzed with overwhelming, suffocating fear. I just sat there for months in that fear until my husband started saying, "You know, if you're not going to do this, you really need to think about getting a job because we still need an additional $1,000 a month." I had this list of things I needed money for, and yet I sat for months and months. I started reading personal development books because that's what my sponsor recommended. My sponsor recommended a book, *Stairway to the Top,* which really inspired me. That book showed me how to take a few steps, one step at a time. However, I still just sat there—no step taking for me.

My fear was baffling because I was not shy. I could go into a room, talk to everybody, and walk out with new friends. I knew I had a friendly and warm personality along with earning top sales honors in the past. I wasn't sure what this new fear was about, and the only thing I could come up with was that this industry was taboo, not the norm. Was I afraid of people asking me the pyramid scheme question and asking me why I didn't I just go back and sell computers for IBM? I started justifying my fear, and that kept me paralyzed. That's when my sponsor did something smart. He asked me to go see the top money earner in the company that I spoke of earlier, who called me out on being too prissy. Allow me to share a little more of this story. I drove by myself to this meeting, and it was two hours away. I went by myself because who would I ask to go with me? I still had not told anyone what I was doing, and I was already six months in. When I got there, the room was full, and I sat in the back. He was exceptionally passionate, caring, and involved in what he was doing. I related to him because of his background. He had two children, and in the beginning his wife was not into what he was doing, but he kept going. He would go to cities to host meetings, and because he didn't have enough money he had to sleep in his car.

He did whatever it took to make it happen. He asked all his colleagues and administrative staff at school to try his products, and they all said no. As the years went by, he was able to leave his teaching job and go into network marketing full-time. Listening to him, something within me shifted. I felt like I could do it too. I also felt worthy of doing it. I decided to do it for myself and my family, and what others thought or said didn't matter. His story moved me out of fear and into full on action. I got over myself with that story, and that is why it is so important to share your story or someone else's as you are getting started.

The next morning, I got up early, and I started making calls. This was back in 1995 when you picked up a phone that felt like 100 pounds and made a phone call. That shift within me caused me to become more confident even though nothing had changed on the outside. I had changed on the inside, so my voice now carried more confidence and passion. I caught the vision of what would be possible for me, and I got started. I didn't know how I was going to do it. I didn't know anything more than I knew the day before, but I knew this: I now had the drive and passion. No matter what, I was doing this thing. The fear was still there watching and waiting to bait me, but what I discovered about fear is that you can treat it as a tool to drive you. When I feel fear coming up, I know that I'm about to embark on something new, something different, something more. If fear isn't present, then I'm being complacent, I'm not stepping out of my zone, I'm not doing anything new, I'm not going to increase that commission check, I'm not going to change lives. Fear is never gone. It's always there with you. I use fear to drive my purpose. It tells me that I am onto something big. I talk to it. I'll say, "Fear, I can feel you, I can sense you, and I appreciate you. You are telling me that I'm going somewhere big, so I thank you. I'm doing this, I'm going to take a step" and then I start.

As we move up in the business and are labeled as leaders, an element of fear sets in. We start to question, "How did I get here? How am I supposed to act? What does a leader do?" Most of us are raised in a work environment and the so-called leaders in that environment are really managers, so we think of leadership as management, which is the main reason people get stuck in their ranks. We stop doing the things that we did to get to where we are, which are gathering customers and sponsoring distributors. We start to manage our teams instead, which slows the growth of the entire team because your team does what you do.

In this industry, you don't get paid to manage people; you get paid to inspire people to continue to build. As you start to build, it looks like it is easier to manage the people on your team than it is to bring in new people. You soon discover that this is a dead end. People don't want to be managed—they want to be inspired, they want you to lead them. If you are managing, they will also sit down and start to manage. Your rich girl business soon becomes a poor girl business of no one working, everyone managing, and with that there is stalled growth. At every rank of your business, 80 percent of your time should be spent in bringing in new customers and distributors and moving them through the system. The remaining 20 percent of your time should be spent in training and guiding. Most people are flip-flopped on this, and this is the reason their business is in a downward spiral. If you understand this, this can save you a lot of time and energy. We are never too good, too smart, or too rich to stop recruiting. That is the lifeblood of any business.

Success in this industry takes different people different lengths of time. It could take some people six months, it could take some a year, and it could take some ten years to reach certain ranks or promotions. Sometimes, when it seems like it's taking too long, people panic and wonder what's wrong. Their fear can be so strong that they don't even reach out to somebody for a while. They often wait too long before they reach out for support because they are scared. I'd love for all readers to understand that if you feel the fear, reach out to someone fast. It's important. Uncover what is behind that fear.

Some people fear being a one-hit wonder—having some initial success, and then it stops. They wonder whether maybe they just got lucky. This is just fear talking along with your poor girl self. It's so self-sabotaging that it could shut you down. It can take you backward. Then your passion level becomes so low that fear becomes overwhelming. It's sort of like falling in love. You know when you first meet someone and become so enamored that you pretty much forget everyone else around you? After a while, you become complacent. You get used to things. You think that things can never be any better. Over time, the passion can wane, just like in a marriage when the honeymoon is over. It's the same with this business. It's comfortable when the calmness sets in, but we've still got to bring in new customers, new distributors, and develop new ways to stay passionate. This is where personal development becomes your greatest ally. Whether it's podcasts, books, or seminars, you've got to maintain the passion by taking time and putting it into personal development. I'm always doing what I call an "awareness check." I check in with myself when I am feeling fear. Why am I feeling this way? What is really going on here? I encourage you to do this awareness check whenever you get to a place where you're not moving in the direction that you want. I also take my journal with me on the road everywhere I go. I write down what I'm thinking and analyze the thoughts behind the talk. Nobody ever sees this, but it's a valuable tool for me. When you are having self-limiting thoughts, write them down and ask yourself, "Is this really true about me?" It's amazing how much you grow professionally when you become more self-aware.

When you become more aware of your own fears, you will be better able to sense when others are experiencing fear, and that's one of the important skills you can develop in this industry. One technique I use that works very well when I sense someone on my team is dealing with fear is this. I'll say, "Look, you've got sixty seconds. Just rant, just tell me like it is. What's going on?" Usually, they'll say things such as, "I just don't think I can do it. I can't get anybody. Nobody wants to be my customer. My team is not working." After sixty seconds I tell them their time is up and ask them to take a breath. Then I ask, "Are you ready to do something about it?" One of two things is going to happen. The first possibility is that they're going to continue to tell me all the reasons why they can't do it, and that tells me they're not ready to do something about it and that they are not open to receiving coaching. I'll say, "Well, look, when you're ready, when you're truly ready to do something about it, why don't we get back together?" I have coached enough to know that no matter what I say, it's not going to resonate with them at this moment because they are too caught up in what is not working. They can't hear what I am going to coach them on. And the second possibility is that sometimes they are ready because they will take a deep breath and say something such as, "Yes, I am so over being stuck here." Then you know that they're open, and you can start down that path of finding out what's really going on.

Fear does not have to be ugly. Fear tells you, "You need to do something big, something really big, and you need to pay attention." You can harness that fear because it is powerful energy, and it can help you move through things.

Again, talk to fear, "Okay, you're here, I'm talking to you. I can sense you; I know we're getting ready to do something big. But I trust you, I trust myself; we're going to be okay." Fear wants to keep you complacent. It wants to keep you in the same spot. Its number-one job is to protect. When you were little it protected you from running into traffic or putting your hand on a hot stove. As we grow, our problems are bigger, fear becomes stronger, but it doesn't have to win.

ASK YOURSELF:

What do you fear?

What is holding you back?

What keeps you from being the best you?

Are you ready to do something about it?

_____

_____

_____

_____

_____

_____

_____

_____

_____

_____

_____

_____

_____

_____

_____

_____

_____

_____

_____

_____

_____

_____

_____

_____

_____

_____

_____

Chapter 9

Giving and Receiving

"Giving is the way of the Rich Girl."
—Pam Sowder

How do you feel about giving back to others? Do you incorporate it into your life and business? You may wonder why I wrote a chapter on giving and receiving, but experience has taught me that if we do not get these two important elements in our life in place, then we can sacrifice our dreams.

Let us discuss giving first. I remember being a little girl in church and seeing that people didn't feel that they could put something in the offering, and I knew my parents struggled with that too. I felt heartbroken about that. What if I just gave a nickel at church? Would I embarrass myself? Would it make a difference? So, when I thought about giving back, many not-so-good feelings came up, because I was thinking from a place of lack. I felt like the poor girl. It affects every area of your life living in this place of lack.

Many of us have felt this way. We've all heard that money is hard to make, so why would we give it away? Why doesn't everyone get up and take care of their own? I can't give back, because I can hardly feed myself. Growing up, I bought into those beliefs because they served me. I could keep all the money to myself. Come on you've been there too.

I knew I had to change my mindset on giving back, but I needed to do my research, so I went to the best source I know: the Bible. This scripture is something that anyone can learn to love to live by. Luke 6:38 says: "Give, and you will receive. Your gift will return to you in full—pressed down, shaken together to make room for more, running over, and poured into your lap." Try it. It works!

I don't know about you, but I can get really excited about this because anything that will be pressed down, shaken together to make room for more along with running over and then poured into your lap sounds like a winning plan to me. This is the way of the rich girl. However, there is one caveat: you must come from a place of not wanting anything in return, as the gift you give is the gift—it's the love that you felt in the giving. I find that it is pressed down, it shook my heart, and was poured back into my lap with love.

Once we started giving back and giving back in a big way, a plethora of emotions came as well as more opportunities. We give back today for the most part without telling anyone unless we feel it will move others to give. It is exhilarating when you give without expecting any acknowledgment back. Once again, we consulted the Bible for help, and we found direction in Matthew 6:2: "So when you give to the needy, do not announce it with trumpets, as the hypocrites do in the synagogues and on the streets, to be honored by men."

I find for us we can give more freely because the giving is not to receive anything from it other than a warm heart and knowing that we just made a difference. Dave taught me this. He has such a warm heart for giving. He is such a humble man. We feel such an immense amount of gratitude that we can give. However, no matter how you give, it's important to establish giving early on even if it is a nickel, time, a smile, or a bottle of water. Give from a place of love and gratitude. You will receive way more than you realize. Go ahead and give it a try. That is the only way you will know what I am talking about.

One of the things that I would hope that most of you would consider doing is giving back to yourselves in the form of mindset, health, and wealth. We think working hard and giving must be a grind, and that it can't possibly be fun. We think making money, working out, and eating healthy must be painful. But when you are full-on participating in life, being present, all of it can be fun. The fun is in getting excited about your workout, your meal, or creating wealth. The fun will propel you forward, and more people will want to join you because most are not having fun doing what they do every day.

Let's talk about the network marketing industry and the best way to give back to your team. You sign people up in your business. Some of them disappear. I call it ghosting. Ghosting is breaking off a relationship by stopping all communication and contact with the partner without any apparent warning or justification, as well as ignoring the partner's attempts to reach out. Sometimes ghosting happens within the first 24 hours and sometimes years later. No matter the length of time, Ghosting can hurt. You gave of your time, energy, and knowledge. What I have found is that it's okay. You still gave, which means your pressing down and running over is still going to happen. I used to take this too personally. I thought I must be a bad leader, sponsor, or person in general. So I asked myself, "Did you do the absolute best for them?" And the answer was yes. That gave me permission to move on. If I did the best possible job for them and they ghosted, then that is the best for me and my business because they got out of the way for new business. It's never what we think. It's always for our benefit.

I always give of my knowledge, time, and expertise. That is also a way of giving back. It doesn't cost you anything financially, but you are giving back to people. Knowledge and time are valuable commodities. I believe that giving of your time is one of the greatest gifts. People want to know that you care, and when you give them time, you show that you care. One of the things that we want to be aware of is giving to the people that truly want it. We sometimes want our business to grow so badly that we give to people who are not willing to do the work on their own. They don't show up, and they don't acquire new business, so we think if we just give them more, they will do more. That form of giving will only cause you distress. Figure out very quickly if they are here to really get into the game by giving them small things to accomplish, and see whether they accomplish them. This will tell you whether they are serious or not.

One of the biggest mistakes I made in the industry is that I would get people's customers and give them distributors. I wanted to build fast, but it created a big set of problems because right up front I was subconsciously telling them that I didn't think they could do it. I disrespected them by thinking this. And an even bigger issue came up, they began to expect it. I soon realized this was not the right way to be giving because it was selfish. I wanted to grow no matter what, and I was using people for that growth. As I said earlier, I was thinking of them as "spots." It might work in the short term, but it won't last. It creates entitlement, and people never learn to build their own business. It also doesn't teach them the right skills, and they start giving away customers and distributors to build their team, and no one can keep that up. Take the time to teach them how to build. At the beginning it takes longer; however, the long-term effects are worth the additional time and energy: you have less people leaving because they will feel proud of their own work, and you will not get burnt out.

Giving is a very personal issue for all of us. We all must figure out what is most important to us when it comes to giving. It's a process. If you are starting with a grateful heart, then you're already halfway there. If it doesn't feel good or right, don't do it. Wait until it does, or you will put yourself in the scarcity mode, and things will start to unravel for you.

I taught my children from a very early age how to take care of themselves, such as laundry. It took weeks for them to get it right; however, once they did, they were very proud of themselves, and I didn't have to do their laundry again—double win! It was well worth those weeks. It's the same with distributors in the beginning. It takes a little time. It takes some patience. Everyone starts differently with different skills, and guiding them softly through it is your gift to them. You want them to be serious about their business, so you must teach them from that place. If you have a four o'clock call, then you show up on time. If they don't show up, then go find them. Let them know that you showed up and that you expected them to as well. If you're doing an in-home or online opportunity meeting, show up early to set things up. This shows you and them that you are serious about your business. It speaks volumes to everyone, and it especially speaks volumes to you. You have got to set the stage on what you want in this business, and how you do anything is how you do everything. Always show up full on ready to win.

This is what duplication is all about. Teach others correctly so they will teach those below them correctly. When I look at leadership and I look at the people who are top earners, I see that they have learned the skills on giving back to their teams the right way. They respect their business and their team, and they are teaching the right ways to build. You want to give to your team by teaching them how to "fish."

Of course, you're not going to influence everyone, and that's okay. You wish you could, but some are just not ready. Just give with a loving heart, and do not expect anything in return. If you're expecting something, that's not the right way to give. Does somebody you know need a pat on the back? Give it. Most people love it when they are told they're doing a good job.

There's a great book called *The 5 Love Languages: The Secret to Love that Lasts* by Gary Chapman. It talks about the different ways people give and like to receive. Some of us give with words of affirmation such as, Good job, and some show love through acts of service. It really helps if you understand the "love language" of the people closest to you and the people you work with. Then you know how to most effectively give to them.

Try to have fun with giving. Enjoy it and experiment. Try to figure out what peoples' love languages are. Take some action right now. Just give someone a kind word or a smile, and watch what happens. I've heard stories about people close to suicide and someone smiled at them or gave them a kind word, and they changed their mind. That's powerful.

Feedback is one of the most valuable gifts we can give. We must find gentle ways to give it—ways that preserve dignity. I've learned that the "feedback sandwich" is a great way to do this. The way to give someone negative feedback is to "sandwich" it between two positives. For example, you could mention something the person has done that's great. Then address the problem, and follow that with another piece of positive feedback.

Science provides a lot of evidence that giving creates changes in the brain and helps us live healthier, longer lives. Helping others is hardwired into our brains, but sometimes we must shake our brains up a little to make it a habit. It's also important to remember that giving doesn't always feel great. It can leave us feeling depleted and empty. So, how do you give in ways that keep you wanting to give more? I think if you give from the place of your passions, you can't help but feel energized. The amount of love you put into your giving matters. Giving of your time doesn't always mean you have to devote your whole life to jobs in service. Time is one thing we all have, but a minute is sometimes all someone needs. So give from what you already have. Don't ever let anyone guilt-trip you into giving. If you are giving only to meet someone else's expectations, you are going to feel drained. You will not feel the joy that giving should provide.

The key to giving is to find the approach that works best for you, and then do it from a place of abundance and joy. When you do this, you can't help but find joy, happiness, and meaning in your life.

Receiving is just as important as giving, and for some of us it's even more difficult because we come from a place of not enough. *I don't deserve this raise. I don't deserve this good life. I don't deserve to have more.* I had to learn how to receive in my life and to be grateful for what seemed like the smallest of gifts; however, if we don't receive the smallest, how are we going to receive the biggest? When I was in seventh grade, a boy gave me my first compliment that I could remember that didn't come from a family member, and I did what most of us do: I tried to explain it away. I tried to give the compliment over to the outfit that I was wearing. He stopped me in mid-sentence and said, "Just say thank you!" Wow. Just say thank you. That's it. He gave, I received. I have never forgotten that valuable lesson.

In our daily activities receiving and being grateful will take us beyond our wildest dreams because it places us in a very powerful position. It places us in thankfulness, which opens our hearts for more.

I also struggled with gifts—giving and receiving. It just wasn't something that our family freely gave of, and I believe it was because we were lacking in money, and so very little was given in the way of personal gifts. However, that was also with compliments and feeling thankful, which led to some issues of lack. It is something that I have worked on most of my life: to freely give and receive.

When we say thank you for even the smallest of checks and are grateful for that money, we are open to receiving more. If we belittle it, we close it off. We think in lack with this type of attitude, and we must turn this around. When I received my first check of $15.78, I was deeply thankful that the company paid. I worked hard for that check and knew that if I kept going, my check would increase. I knew that the giving of my time and energy would eventually show up in a bigger check. We must believe in order to receive.

Most of us have never been in a commission-based business or opportunity. We are brought up that if you work for $10 an hour and you work ten hours, you would earn $100. So we are really stepping out in faith that if we work, work, work that it will pay off at some point. I always tell people that are new to the industry that in the beginning you will put in more time than you can possibly imagine for what looks like little financial reward; however, over time, the reward comes, and over time the work is less and the rewards are higher. It is the opposite of what we have been taught but way more rewarding. Trust must be there along with gratefulness and a strong belief in yourself. I also have experience that what you say over your team and your business is your form of advertisement, even though most people will never physically hear your words. Are you saying or having thoughts that your team doesn't work, that your check is too small, that your customers quit, that the products don't work, and that that no one is joining? If you continue "advertising" this over your business, you will continue to receive these same things. Start advertising that you have a team with a strong work ethic, that your check is growing bigger and bigger every month, that your customers are loyal, that the products are producing the best results, and that you have more people joining daily than ever before. What team do you think people want to be a part of when they sense this form of advertising? The one in lack with the poor girl mentality or the one in prosperity with the rich girl mentality. These words and thoughts affect your attitude, and your attitude affects your business. Advertise what you want out of life and your business, and stand firm in receiving it.

ASK YOURSELF

Think back on some of the ways that giving or the lack of giving affected you as a child. Are you still holding on to those beliefs?

Have you given at times only expecting to receive?

Do you value what others have given you?

Where or who would you like to give back to?

Do you need to work on receiving?

What is your advertisement over your business?

Chapter 10

Is It Being Done to You or for You?

"When you feel like you're drowning in life, don't worry—
your Lifeguard walks on water."
—AUTHOR UNKNOWN

Look at the title of this chapter. What does that ignite for you? I think there are people who go through life thinking everything is being done to them. They are victims. They think nothing is working for them and the world is out to get them. When you think that everything is being done for you, it's called conscious living. It's all about awareness. It's about wondering how you can learn from what happens. How can you use it to grow, to take more responsibility for your own life?

For me, this means that if I can be conscious of what's happening and look for the miracle in it, the wisdom in it, then I am no longer a victim of circumstances. I am now in control. I am powerful. It might be the worst thing possible at that moment, but somehow, I can turn it around and use it for growth. How many times have you read about people who say that a serious disease or accident was the best thing that ever happened to them? That accident or disease ended up being a turning point in their lives.

I hear this often in the network marketing industry; people will ask, "Why is my team not motivated? Why is my check the same? Why is it not growing?" No matter what your age or background, you can always overcome those victim thoughts. I have proven to myself that by changing my thoughts, I can change my body, my income, and my relationships. You can do it too if you look at it from a place of awareness—that true power that you possess within you. When you decide it's hard to succeed, it'll be hard. When you decide you can do it, then you will do it.

You get to decide what you want your business to look like. And, know that it is your responsibility to generate wealth, awareness, and growth, so make the decision on what you want to create and how you want to create it along with how you want to live each day.

Based on these decisions, get to work. There are no limits. Life and network marketing are designed so that you can achieve whatever you want. You can have the lifestyle along with the freedom. If you have the inspiration along with your why deep within you, then any action that comes from that place is what will take you through any obstacle in achieving your dreams. That's when everything begins to open for you. All of it comes to you because you're taking inspired action. Fall in love with the process, even though it might not be the thing you enjoy the most. I wrapped people with our crazy wrap product in every place imaginable: abdomens, legs, arms, necks, faces, and places I don't care to mention. Back in the day, we even measured those areas to show results. It was not the most pleasant thing to do; however, I changed my attitude and made a bold statement to myself that if I was going to be doing this, I might as well have fun with it. I started laughing with everyone, enjoying the process, and you know what? The results I started getting were profound. The people that I wrapped wanted to be a part of the company because of their results but most importantly because we were having fun together.

I've watched people work long hard hours from a place of scarcity and judgment, and their business might take off for a hot minute, but it eventually deep dives because of the negative energy attached to what they were doing. Which one do you think works better in the long run? Which one is more fun? Which one is more profitable? You know the answer to that because you have worked in life both ways. Change your attitude, and your check changes.

At the beginning of my career, I came from the not-much-fun place. I thought competitively, and I was judgmental. I thought I had to do it all. Nobody else could be like me because they weren't like me. I'm just going to do it all myself, and I pretty much did. This caused me to have a disbelief in people and eventual burnout. I never felt good at the end of the day or when I got a promotion, because there was no one there to celebrate with me. Who would want to hang out with me, anyway? Boy, did I need to grow up. As I stated earlier, I learned very quickly that these spots I was filling were human beings, not a quick check. I didn't build relationships because I thought they were going to quit anyway, so why would I want to get close? That's what happens when you build a network marketing business from a poor girl perspective with a scarcity mindset. You don't have fun, and no one else around you does either.

You must inspire your team by being inspired yourself. You can't teach them how to get their own customers or distributors if you don't coach them and believe in them. You teach them the system and show them how to use the data and training your company provides. You take time, and in the beginning it can seem as if it's taking a long time, but if you teach them well, it will be time well spent because they will be able to teach it to someone else. That's what duplication is all about. Your business will explode, and at the end of each day you will feel proud of your accomplishments.

You are also duplicating relationships. You are duplicating the fun, the community, the joy in every day. Fall in love with every aspect of your day, and money will flow so fast that you will be blown away. And at the end of it, when you get that promotion and you're standing there, there's your team—they're crying, and they are really excited for you. They can't believe that they were part of it. Everything is moving smoothly and with such precision, and you can feel proud that you created it! You have become that rich girl.

That's what I want for everyone—to feel proud of who they are, to have their family and relationships intact. I truly believe that you can have it all. I feel and know that because I do. I've done it inspired, and I've done it uninspired. I've done it like a bulldog, and I've done it where people are more important than sales. I'll take the inspired way any day! We all want the financial rewards, but the friendships and relationships become way more valuable.

When we start seeing that success, the first thing that happens is we start doubting we can maintain it. I'd like to tell you the story of one of my favorite people, Carla, who is a top money earner with our company and has been for over a decade. Carla and I were on a training trip together outside the U.S. We were groggy because of the time change, and it was 6:00 a.m. when we had this conversation while waiting to take a car to the airport. Carla just seemed very down on herself, so I finally asked her what was going on. She told me that she had reached the number one earner position in our company many months before, and instead of feeling overjoyed, she felt the opposite, all because she didn't receive the recognition that she felt she should have. Carla was looking for love in all the wrong places. Her thoughts were so self-sabotaging and destructive that her check took a deep dive, and I mean it went from five figures down to three. Carla was playing out the poor girl.

How could this possibly happen? Think about the dynamics of that. How does her team know what she was feeling? This sense of lack came from not getting recognition, which equated to, "I must not be good enough because no one recognized me." When you are on fire for your business, your team can feel it just as they can sense when you are not. Your negative attitudes show up in your words and actions. Carla's team went dormant because she went dormant, and she stopped doing what she did to get the big check. I talked to Carla and told her, "If you're expecting anyone outside of you to acknowledge you, to give you the accolades that you want, you're going to be disappointed most of the time."

Don't expect recognition to come from the outside because it will never seem it's enough, and it is over quickly. If it does, that's awesome, and you should be proud of that moment and soak it up. You're going to be on that stage one day with everybody shouting your name, but when the lights go down and the cheering fades away and you are all alone, you've got to know that it was great; however, it's back to work time. Bask in it but not too long. If you are not filling yourself with your own acceptance and love, you could end up losing it all. The good news is Carla took this to heart and got back to work, and her check got back up and well beyond what is was before. She became the rich girl and has maintained that for years.

Isn't that interesting, that we have the power to affect our entire business with our thoughts that therefore affect our actions?

We all want admiration, love, and the attention. We all deserve it. I hope that we can get better at giving and receiving it with true gratitude. If we operate from a place of always wanting the cheers, we are going to be disappointed. Get great at giving back to yourself in the way of rewards and self-care. You will win every time when you take on this practice.

I look forward every year to our company convention. It is a time of celebration and acknowledgement. I want those moments for you every day, not just once a year! Every day is a day to celebrate. Being present means loving each moment as it is, whether you are at a conference or just sitting at home and posting on social media. Even if you get a no from a potential customer, that's a cause for celebration too because dang gone it, you reached out to them. You asked. Don't be crushed daily by what's happening or what appears to be happening on the outside because if you are doing the thing persistently, the results will show up.

Too many people have the experience of going to a convention, getting all fired up, and then coming home and doing nothing with the knowledge and enthusiasm they gained. How do you maintain your level of celebration every day? By surrounding yourself with the right people and by reading and listening to inspirational material every day, especially when you find yourself dipping into those negative thoughts. This is the way to learn to self-correct quickly. Don't expect to wake up every day raring to go and feeling 100 percent fired up. It takes work, especially at the beginning until it becomes a habit. Put on some upbeat music and dance. Nothing changes our state faster than music; move that body, and everything moves. And like me, many of you are parents, so when I was down, I would go look at my children while they were sleeping, and that moved me into full-on action because they were and still are my why.

Let's go back to the title of this chapter. What do you think? Is life being done to you or for you? Are you in charge of your own destiny (the answer should always be yes), or are you a victim of bad circumstances? The language of victimhood is always the language of self-defeat and lack. It is the language of the poor girl.

Creator language (or the idea that life happens *for* you) is the language of self-determination, improvement, and opportunity—even when things are not going the way you would like them to, they will eventually show you wisdom. This is the language of the rich girl.

ASK YOURSELF:

Is your language the language of the rich girl or the poor girl?

Are you allowing life to get in your way?

Are you limiting yourself?

Are you waiting for others to recognize and reward you?

Are you willing to give yourself the self-care and love that you so deserve?

Chapter 11

The Cursed How

"The only true wisdom is in knowing you know nothing."
—SOCRATES

HOW! How do I do this business? Where do I start? Please tell me, how, how, how! I would go to meeting after meeting and ask the top money earners this very question. I would tell them that their talk inspired me, but how did they *do* it? They would always look at me with this weird look of "Heck, I just did it." But in the beginning of my career that wasn't enough. I was having some success but not on the level that they were, and I wanted that, so there must be an answer. Consequently, I kept going to meetings, and I kept asking. I thought there must be a hidden secret, and they are all keeping it to themselves. I had to find out this secret to these hows that were plaguing me.

One night I was having dinner with the top money earner in my first company. I was fortunate enough to be sitting directly across from him when the woman to his left started talking negatively. He let her go on for a few minutes and then finally looked at her and said, "You have to leave right now, unless you can sit and not say another word!" He honestly didn't say it that nicely, but I thought I would fluff it up a bit since this is my book. It was very confusing to me that she was talking like that because I thought she should be as excited as I was to be sitting at the table with him.

Wouldn't everyone want to soak up everything he had to say because at that time, he was earning over a million a month, and yes, I wrote it right, a month. I wanted him to tell me how he did it because if anyone had the secret, he did. So I asked him, and his answer was shocking. He said, "First of all, guard your mind; never allow anyone or anything to get into your head of what you don't want." Gulp, there was his reason for telling the woman to leave. Then, he said, "I just did it. I started. Some things worked, and some didn't. I took the noes with the yeses. Either one was okay with me. I knew that the noes meant they were not ready, and therefore they were not going to waste my time. The yeses meant, let's play ball. Some would stay. Some would quit. Either way was good." Then he said something that totally blew me away. He said, "Three solid people stayed and built three strong legs under me, and that is what accounted for my millions." Three people. He had recruited over 100, but three people stayed and built that, which accounted for his millions. I found the secret: "Just start!"

So I started over again at that moment with a new attitude. Some things worked. Some didn't. Some people stayed, most quit, but I never did, and that was the most important thing. If you don't quit and you learn the necessary skills by starting and paying attention to what works and what doesn't, you will create your dream business. I also learned to not allow the negative chatter of the poor girl inner bully to affect me for longer than a hot minute because I wanted it, and I was going to have it. I wanted to be that rich girl, that girl who knew that I didn't need to know how I was going to get there, but I did need to know where I was going and why I was going and that I was not willing to give up on my dreams.

Today, I train people to understand that you don't have to impress anyone with your skill or business acumen when you are pursuing your dreams. All you've got to do is jump in and take the steps forward to do it—one step at a time, day after day! Stay confident and consistent, and you'll get there. Will you make a mistake or two? Of course you will. We all do. But mistakes are the foundation for huge growth, and every business owner makes them.

I've since met so many people along the way who were just like me. They were stay-at-home moms or grandmothers who had no experience at all in business who are just killing it—they're doing amazing things! First, you must know the reason that you are going to start—your why—and then you get up every day and take action.

Let me share with you a quick story about GoGo, a grandmother we met while on a mission trip in Africa who takes care of her seven grandchildren, who are obviously her why. You could just tell after meeting her that she gets up every day not wondering how she is going to feed her family but instead wakes up and takes action based on what she has right in front of her. They live in what we would consider the worst living conditions imaginable for any family. They are without adequate clothing, a bathroom, and running water. The day we met her, I couldn't believe the joy and gratitude on her face when we brought her family food and the pride she took as she showed us around her home, which had dirt floors, a few chickens, and a small garden.

As we walked away from her home, our stomachs were upside down. We couldn't say a word. None of us had ever experienced such poverty along with such joy. We were half-way down her small mountain when we heard her voice and saw her running after us with two small bags of beans as a gift. She gave us something that was so precious to her—food—to show her gratitude to us. I've never had such generosity bestowed on me before. We thought we'd helped her, but what she gave us was even bigger in return: pure joy and love.

My point in telling this story is that at the beginning of your network marketing journey you may get up each day not knowing how the day will progress, but you continue to take action based on what you do know and most importantly your reason for doing it. GoGo taught us to go. Just go. Get up and do the thing whatever that might be, for the day. When I truly understood that I didn't need to know how I was going to accomplish my dream but also understood that the hows were no longer a reason for me to not get started, I eliminated them as an excuse. I'm committed to just doing it and asking questions when I need help.

What about you? Are you willing to eliminate the negative self-talk and get rid of the need to know *how* in order to move forward? Don't get stuck in the "I can'ts," or the "I don't know hows" because if you stay there, you'll never start. Action is the key to any great business! Think of the most successful entrepreneurs you know, and you'll see that it's not about how smart they are but how persistent and action-oriented they are! Work your business, and don't focus on the how. Learn as you go!

ASK YOURSELF:

Do you use not knowing how to start as a reason not to?

Do you go from book to book or meeting to meeting looking for the answer on how to start?

Does getting a no stop you?

Do you now understand that you have to just start?

Chapter 12

Let Go of the Wheel

Jesus, take the wheel
Take it from my hands
'Cause I can't do this on my own
I'm letting go
So give me one more chance
And save me from this road
I'm on Jesus, take the wheel
—CARRIE UNDERWOOD

As I was preparing to drive from my home in Virginia to a meeting in Charlotte, North Carolina, on a sunny winter morning, Dave came in with the weather report and said it looks like snow is on its way. Of course, I didn't listen. Isn't that just like us girls? We don't listen when someone, even those who love us, give us feedback to protect us. We forge ahead without thinking of the consequences. I had no intention of not traveling that day because I had things to do. I was going to this meeting that was being hosted by one of my new distributors, and he was excited about me coming and sharing the opportunity, plus the sun was shining, so game on. I took off in my Volvo wagon and headed down I81 for the mountains of North Carolina. Everything was going well until I reached Radford, and then the snow started falling with flakes the size of nickels. I drove another 30 minutes and knew that I needed to turn around. I81 is an interstate that I have traveled on most of life. I knew it well, and one of those things that I knew well is that it is always full of 18 wheelers, and they own that road no matter what the weather is.

I started moving slow because I was starting to shake with fear. I am not that great of a driver in snow, so I thought the slower, the better. I was in the left lane when I hit black ice that quickly took hold of my tires. I looked in my rear-view mirror, and in full sight was an 18 wheeler that was coming right behind me while the spin on the ice took place. It seemed like an hour as I write about it, but it was a matter of seconds when the full spin took place, and I was losing control. That is when I heard a distinct male voice say, "Let go of the wheel." Now most of you are probably thinking, "Yeah, right." But then again if you've ever had a supernatural experience, you know it can happen. Well this was the first time for me.

But a peace came over me that is truly hard to describe, but it felt like calm, love, and warmth, all at the same time. I knew that I was going to be okay, no matter what, so I let go of the wheel. I put my arms up in the air, and my car spun around several times and then went down a very steep ditch on the right-hand side of the road and graciously flipped over. I sat in that ditch dangling upside down. Think about that for a minute. What if you saw someone spinning out of control on black ice with a small smile on their face and their arms up in the air? You would think that person had lost their mind, but it gets even more interesting.

Within minutes of flipping over, I heard a knock on the passenger-side door, and there were two men standing there who looked exactly alike. They were rather small, without any hair, and had the most beautiful blue eyes and the brightest of smiles. They asked me, "Are you okay?" I said, "Yes, I think so." They told me to be sure and hold one hand up on the ceiling of the car while I unbuckled my seat belt so that I wouldn't hurt my neck. So I did that and scooted myself back around. Then they asked, "Can you open your door?" There was a lot of snow piled up beside my door, so I said, "I think so!" I tried the door, and it opened, so I told them that, but of course they could see, so they said, "Okay, we can go now."

I pleaded with them to stay, but by the time I stepped out of the car they were gone, and this was within a minute or two at the most. I couldn't understand how they got away so quickly. I heard a shout coming from the highway, and a state trooper was shouting down to me asking me how I was, and said that he saw the whole thing. I asked him where the two men who helped me went, and he said, "Miss, there was no one here." Now, it's difficult for me to write this without tearing up because I remember it as vividly as if it had happened yesterday.

"There are no footprints in the snow," he offered. I walked around to the passenger side of the car, and he was right—there were not any footprints. I was still in so much shock from the accident that I didn't start to question it until I got home. I told a few friends and family members about it, but most just couldn't comprehend it, so I started to think I was delusional. However, now I know I wasn't. I heard that voice and can still hear it today, "Let go of the wheel." And I know those two men were there to help me, and they must have been my guardian angels.

Look, I am a wife, mother, grandmother, friend, and businesswoman like almost everyone else, and I work hard on my business just like everyone else, and I can't explain what I heard or saw, but I do know that it happened. There were two very kind men, and they helped me out of that car. I can still hear and see them clearly, and it's been over a decade since this happened.

This has brought such peace to me over this past decade. Whenever I feel overwhelmed or in need of an answer, I simply let go and let God take over. I have never in my life felt such profound peace as I did in that moment of spinning on black ice. What if we all approached our business with our hands up in surrender and let Jesus take the wheel? It requires faith and a belief beyond understanding.

Instead of being in a moment of sheer terror, it became one of calmness. I simply allowed God to do His work. I feel truly blessed by this, and I am not sure if I would be here today had I disobeyed that command. Whenever you feel overwhelmed, stressed, out of balance, simply get quiet and ask God to step in. He is there for you if you will only ask.

Network marketing has caused me to grow beyond what I thought was possible for me. It has challenged me in a myriad of ways. I've had to get over my self-defeating thoughts of worthlessness and lack while continuing to work on me daily. I could not do it without the people who have been here for me and those who continue to show up. I read, I listen, and I pray. I get quiet and ask, "What do you want to do today, God? I am here for you." And I feel his love and presence all around me. Life is such a blessing, and we are fortunate that we get this chance to not only change our lives but also the lives of those around us.

I work diligently on making sure that I am surrounded by the right people. In the beginning of building my business I thought that anyone who was interested could be a part of my inner circle; however, I quickly realized that this is not playing it smart. It is not judging someone on anything other than what they really want in life and whether that matches with what I want. It means all are welcome, and you will get the benefit of my knowledge through the team trainings and events; however, we might not be a fit now for anything more.

Guard your mind as you would guard your children while allowing them to explore and play but guiding them with the wisdom that you have learned over time. My mother taught me a ton about this. She once discovered notes written to me by a young girl in middle school whom I knew I should not be hanging around, but something about her was intriguing. She seemed exceptionally open and fearless with a sense of reck-lessness. We have all had friends like this, and more than once we ended up in some sort of trouble. Mom came to me with the notes and asked me if this is who I wanted to be like, and I started crying and said, "No, but she is fun in a crazy way." Mom then told me what that "fun" could turn into, so I never hung out with her again. I am so glad that she found those notes, because I know that had I continued to hang out with this girl, I would have been in circumstances and places that I shouldn't be in. Our notes now come in the form of messages, so I look at my text messages and social media messages along with posts and ask myself whether this is someone or some group that I should be spending my time with.

We must look at who we want to become and find those attributes in others and then surround ourselves with those who have them, whether it is someone who is alive today or deceased, through the books and audios that they have left behind. I read and listen to those who have gone before me as well as those who are here with us today; however, I am also aware that not everything that they say or do is always true for me. Question what you read and who you listen to and ask yourself, "Is this true for me?" or "Is this how I want to be or who I want to become?"

For those who become a part of your team, know that they may be there for a season or for life, and whichever one is what it is. That it is not for you to question. So I give to all with that understanding. I protect my inner circle knowing that it is most important because thoughts, ideas, and suggestions that come from others can get within us and cause us to do destructive things as well as beneficial things. I trust my intuition and listen to it without question so that not only can I remain open to new opportunities and people but also know that some things or people are just not right for me and where I am going.

The life of the rich girl is a fulfilling life. It is full of wonder and opportunities. It is growth that is never ending, which means you will not get bored as your life is always one of adventure and expansion. Be open to endless possibilities in all areas of your life. Give yourself grace as you go through your journey, and know that I appreciate the opportunity to come into your life if only in the sharing of this book. Be open to never-ending dreams, and know that you are profoundly loved. Be the rich girl.

ASK YOURSELF:

What do you need to let go of?

What do you want to do today?

What is it that you love about yourself?

Who are the top five people that you surround yourself with?

What and who are you listening to?

What does being the rich girl feel like to you?

Dear reader,

Thank you for reading my story of how I got started in network marketing. It is my desire that the world knows that this is a viable business opportunity for anyone who is open to receiving it. It takes fortitude, decisiveness, focus, and determination. It gives you back exactly what you put into it pressed down, shaken together, and poured into your lap. It is the best calling for someone who loves to give and share while knowing that they too are blessed. It is about more than money. It is about getting rich with gratitude, growth, maturity, skills, business knowledge, and mentors who will serve you to your highest good. Here's to the rich girls who believe that dreams do come true.

If you have thought about joining this industry or already have but you haven't started because of fear, it's never going to feel like the right time or place, but if you are feeling a calling for something more, then you must listen to yourself and know that this is here for you and to take a leap of faith. Just do it.

If you're already in the industry and thriving, hopefully you've learned something valuable from reading my own story. You know how hard it is to push through the fear, juggle all your activities, and overcome every obstacle. But I'm here to tell you that you can. You can do it! Just keep moving and take action every day. Step out in faith, and trust in yourself and your Creator. We've got this!

_____

_____

_____

_____

_____

_____

_____

_____

_____

_____

_____

_____

_____

_____

_____

_____

_____

_____

_____

_____

_____

_____

_____

_____

_____

_____

_____

_____

_____

_____

_____

_____

_____

_____

_____

_____

_____

_____

_____

_____

_____

_____

_____

_____

_____

_____

_____

_____

_____

_____

_____

_____

_____

_____

_____

_____

_____

_____

_____

_____

_____

_____

_____

_____

_____

_____

_____

_____

_____

_____

_____

_____

_____

_____

_____

_____

_____

Ask Pam Questions

Question: I just switched companies and would like to know what the best way is to let my friends and family know why I started with a new company. I am 52 and have never wanted and needed something like this in my life so badly, but I don't know where to start and how to let everyone know.

Answer: *There is such an easy solution to your question, and I am not sure why we feel we must justify the reason for moving in a different direction. I think most of it is because we said our last company was the "be all;" however, you have discovered another company with products that you're just as excited about or even more. What I would recommend that you do is start using the product line. Really get into it, dive into it. Go live on Facebook and share your excitement. Even though this might be something that you're not used to doing, let your friends and family see you using the products, having fun with them, and getting results. People don't buy packaging. They don't buy companies. What they buy is you using the products. That's what they're after. So just start there. Let everybody know that you've discovered a great product and what it does and what it's done for you, and start posting about that.*

Most importantly, don't say, "I've left that company, and I've come to this company" because really, people again are buying you, not the company. You know what? I love that because we don't have to get overly concerned about that. We don't have to say we switched companies, and if someone asks you, say, "Absolutely, I did. I've found a product line that I fell in love with, and I couldn't wait to share it with you."

Question: I just celebrated my one-year anniversary and have ranked up once and want to go even higher. I want to know how I become a better leader.

Answer: *Since your organization is growing right now, and you've been promoted once, that's how you lead your team, with more promotions. You take them with you, you don't step back and try to push or pull them. Your team is young, and it's just getting started, as you are. So the best thing you can do is inspire them by your actions, and those actions are gathering customers and distributors. Keep it really, really simple. And most importantly, utilize the existing upline that you have. The trap that most people fall into is they stop doing what is most important, which is growing their team, and they start managing everyone, which slows everybody down. Growth is your leadership skill right now.*

More than likely, your upline offers a team page that you can put everyone in since you really want to continue to use their team page until you get to the top ranks because your focus should be 100 percent on building your business and taking everybody with you. Keep it simple, have fun, don't stress out on the word leader. *As your business grows, you'll mature more into a leader, and it will happen on its own. Continue to stay plugged in—plugged into your upline, plugged into corporate— while attending as many online trainings and meetings as you can along with personal development. That's the most effective way to learn leadership.*

Question: I've been at the same middle rank for three years and have been in the business for four years. I work a full-time job and promoted to this position in six months. I was building with my sponsor, and we moved fast. After my promotion I coasted and maintained it for a year and a half while building and almost promoting to the next rank position twice but didn't hit the promotion. There are times I question if I can do this or not, but I hang in there and keep my eyes on my why, and that is to pay off the rest of our debt and be a full-time work-at-home mom. Plus, I want to help other families to do the same thing. I've been in corporate America for 20 years and have time to make my dreams happen. How can I do this quickly?

Answer: *Congratulations on being a part of your company for four years and for your promotion. You know what you want, which is to be debt free and a work-at-home mom, which was my why as well. The biggest thing that you can do right now is focus on getting that next promotion. Find out who in your organization is going to go there with you, and make sure that they're 100 percent committed. Focus on that. The income at that level is tremendous and will help you achieve your two goals.*

The biggest mistake that I see almost everyone make is they reach a position in a company and they think it's just going to keep growing on its own without any effort. We all need to participate in our own business daily and not expect people just to build on their own; they're looking at you for leadership, they're looking at you for inspiration. So you've done it, you've experienced that, and you know that it doesn't work to stop and start again and again. Take that knowledge and get on fire for achieving the next rank, even if you have to start completely over. Stop telling the "old story" and create a new one. You can do it, and you can do it in record time because you know what to do. You asked, "How do I build it fast?" You go like your hair is on fire. This business loves speed. Speed is about being consistent with your work, just like running. You don't have the speed that you want when you first start running; however, over time your speed starts to build, and it is not any different here. Go strong. Be consistent. Don't look left or right. Stay in your lane.

Consistency is the key. Every day go after your business. That doesn't mean you spend 24/7 on it. I know you're working and you've got children, so you want to be able to take care of your family, take care of your job right now while you still have that, but every minute that you have free, you want to hone in and focus on your business, which is bringing in new distributors and new customers. That's what you get paid for. That's how you build your team. And, when I think about this, I see so many people get charted out to that next position and just wait for the same people every time to fill it up when you should be sponsoring new—no matter where you're at, you continue to add new people because you could bring somebody in today that would go there with you in record time.

Question: I started by business in 2016 and have a strong why. It's my family. I want to extend that into helping my mom who helps with the younger siblings in my family retire. I've reached the first rank and am determined to reach several higher ranks within the next few months. If it took me a year to reach the first rank, how am I supposed to reach several ranks higher in a couple months? The fire inside me is burning strong to make it happen and yet it hasn't.

Answer: *Over the years I've met a lot of people who have a strong why and a big, big dream, but the actions don't back it up, which means it isn't a dream but a wish. The most important thing here is that you've got to really be honest with yourself and ask yourself, "Has this just been a wish?" You've got your why in place, but I bet that the actions that you're taking daily are not reflecting what the dream truly means to you. You must be consistent and very persistent and not allow what has stopped you in the past to continue to stop you now.*

I was stuck in a fear-based mentality for months on end when I first started in the industry, and I didn't get anywhere because I didn't get bold enough and ask people if they wanted to try the product or if they wanted to take a look at the opportunity. You've got to draw a line in the sand, and you've got to jump over it and go after what you want. Nobody can do that for you. You've got to decide that the whys that you have are worth the efforts that you need to put in. It really is that simple.

Question: I'm a new distributor who's been in for three months. I have my initial customers along with two distributors, and one of those distributors has four customers. I message and post every day but have a hard time signing people. They like my posts and act interested, but then it's crickets. I want to level up so bad and I'm trying so hard. Plus, I'm not good with Instagram. Do you have any suggestions?

Answer: *Well, for one thing, I think you're doing awesome. It took me six months in my first company to even get started,* *let alone sponsor someone. As far as Instagram goes, you will learn that as you go. Most people have very limited knowledge and followers when they start. What I recommend is that you continue to do what you did to get your current customers and distributors because whatever you did, it worked. Just do more of that. Make sure that you're asking more people to be a part of your team, whether it's a customer or distributor, and let them know why you're doing this. Go live on social media and share your story of why you started and how you love the products. The more we share our passion about the products and what the opportunity can bring us and do this consistently, the more successful we will become.*

Also, not every distributor that you bring on board is going to do what you ask them to do to become successful, so don't allow that to get in your way. If some of your distributors don't have their customers, then understand that the business is not for them, and don't take it out on yourself. One of the biggest lessons that I have learned is to not push or pull people along so that I could spend my time working with the ones that really wanted to grow and build.

Share your story every single day, and people can sense that you're going somewhere, and they're going to want to be a part of that journey too. I'm rooting for you.

Question: I'm not a salesperson, and I don't want to bother my friends; however, I have a dream, so how do I build this?

Answer: *I know this feeling very well. I was allowing my excuses of not wanting to be thought of as a salesperson or someone pushing something on my friends and family when I first got started in direct sales. Yes, that was an excuse. You see, I didn't* believe that what I had to offer was good enough, and I didn't want to be known as someone who needed someone's help. I honestly didn't feel that it would work. You know how I know this? Because when I feel that something is great like a movie, a restaurant, or a great recipe, I can't wait to share it. I shout it out to everybody, because I want them to have that same experience, and we love being the one to introduce people to something new. It makes us feel important.

So, I'm not buying it as far as the salesperson thing goes. Here's the deal: get excited about the offer, and what is the offer? Write down everything that you love about the products. How they make you feel. What they taste like. What do you want to gain or lose from taking them? Why did you join as far as the opportunity goes? What are you looking for as far as the extra income coming in? Don't be shy about this. For the first time in your life, admit that you need the money and why you need it. People are also hurting out there and need extra income coming in. Share with your heart and passion, and no one will think you are selling them anything.

We don't teach you to bother your friends, to scam your friends, and we don't teach you sales techniques. I've been taught sales techniques from my IBM experience such as, how to close the deal or how to get the order. What we teach is to fall in love with the aspects of the business and with the products and to share that by being yourself, the self that your friends and family love.

Once I felt the passion for what I wanted and why I wanted it, I had to tell everybody and still do to this every day, because who wouldn't want to feel and look better while making more money from home. Why wouldn't you want to share that with the people that you care about, the people that you love, the *people that know you, that trust you. We don't want you selling. We don't want you to feel like you're selling. Look, you have a gift you are offering, and if someone doesn't want to open it, then let it go for them. We don't want you to change your profile picture or anything like that. We want you to be you with a new zest in life for something more.*

I just read a story about someone that totally blasted one of our top DTS. When they first got started, they defriended them, called them names, and now want to come take a look at the business years later. That's happened to me all the time. No always meant not yet. Nope, not ready yet. As I continued to build, continued to grow, continued to gain confidence, and continued to have success, other people wanted it. So have fun, be friendly, be passionate, get your story out there, be consistent, and you'll have people joining your team whether they become a customer, a distributor, or just a great fan.

Question: Do you feel we are too saturated or we're going to slow down anytime soon?

Answer: *Most people think that companies that have been around for a while become saturated or the people that got in at the beginning make all the money. That's an old myth—it's not true. That's like saying nobody ever needs a new car, or don't buy Amazon stock, when we've seen it rise and rise. Saturation is a myth that people that really don't understand business in general spread around. There are companies that are 60+ years old that continue to grow daily. We attend industry meetings, and we'll meet people in those companies who are just killing it. And that's what you want: a company that you can be with for decades and build a strong business so that it will continue to* *pay you and your family for generations. Companies are always expanding into new countries and new product categories, so there is no end to what is possible. And that's exciting.*

Question: How should you post to attract more people? I've heard some successful distributors mentioned lifestyle posts in addition to product posts. A lot of times these distributors have already made it, so it's easy for them to talk about owning their own time, doing fun things. What do you think lifestyle posts should look like? And what advice would you give to distributors who are still working their full-time jobs and possibly still feeling pinched financially about lifestyle posts and being honest? What are some ways they can share about the opportunity when they haven't felt the increase from it yet?

Answer: *I absolutely love this question because I remember being there not too long ago. When we started building this opportunity, our lifestyle on the outside had not changed for the first ten years. Dave and I lived in the same house, drove the same cars, and Dave only quit his job in 2011. Not much looked like it was changing from the outside; however, we'd paid off all our debt. So on the inside, things were working and getting paid off. I worked my business daily with full-on action without really changing lifestyle because I was working so much; however, I didn't care what others thought. I knew that we were becoming debt free, and my vision of the future was ever present. You know, we didn't have social media back then, so I couldn't show that we cut up credit cards or that we paid off our bills. I could have shared that we no longer had a mortgage or pictures of us spending almost every weekend in the summer at our daughter's softball tournaments. How many of you would love to be able to* *do that? You know, that was costly. We were getting hotel rooms, travel, gas, food. We were spending probably $500 a weekend almost every weekend in the summer, and I am so thankful that we had the opportunity and money to do that.*

So, now what do you do when you first get started and not much is changing? This is all of us; however, our dreams are so big for what we are wanting—so we just start, and we share something as simple as paying for gas with cash or not worrying about the cost of groceries. It's what seems like the small things that are very significant for most people that we need to show. It doesn't have to be a big trip to Hawaii. That's so far-fetched for most people that they can't even fathom that; however, it's the small everyday things that are so important for most of us that is the real struggle. Let's say that you were able to take off on a Tuesday and go to the park with your children. Share that. Do you know how many people are at work that would love to be able to take off on a Tuesday and go to the park with their children? Let's say that you pay for daycare but it's a struggle and how this has helped ease that burden.

Most importantly, talk about your dreams. What are you dreaming for? Build that dream board and put that out there. That's visionary. I encouraged our two children to create their own dream wall in their bedroom. They could put anything up there that they wanted. They either drew or cut pictures out and taped them on the wall of things that they wanted or what they wanted to be able to achieve such as in music or sports. This is very powerful for families because most families don't dream any more.

You can share pictures of purchasing clothes or going on a trip and not worrying about the ice cream. That was important for me to be able to take trips and not worry about how much *an ice cream cone cost. How about a movie or concert that you took your spouse on a date with you, and you paid for the date with the money you earned? Show that you're paying double on a loan. How about paying an extra $1,000 down on a credit card? That's tremendous. You don't have to show the whole card that you cut up, but you paid a lot more on it. Share that you're giving back.*

In other words, it is the everyday life experiences that people really want. And I remember being that mom just wanting to be able to breathe, you know, wanting to be able to buy Dave a gift and not use his money. That was something I couldn't do because I wasn't working. I wanted to really be able to do that, to go out and buy that present, whether it was his birthday or Father's Day or Christmas that I actually paid for it myself. So you could share something as simple as that.

I'll never forget needing a new washing machine, and we just couldn't afford it. So I got a used one. I didn't want to use someone else's washing machine. I wanted a new washing machine. So it's things like that that everybody out there is looking for, it's not the big, big stuff. Eventually they'll be able to get that, but it's those small significant things that people are looking for. So yes, you can start posting every single day from day one. Be proud of these moments. It always starts the same for all of us, so let's make your ending incredible.

As far as the products go, this is very simple. Become a product of the products and share your results. When you first start you don't have results other than your hopes and dreams of what the products will do for you. Take people on this journey with you by going LIVE and sharing how you are making your product, taking your product, and sharing in those experiences. Fall in love with the products, and share your passion for what they are doing for you and those around you. You can always look for others who have a story and share theirs when you first get start-ed. Don't give in to your excuses of not having a story to share. Everyone has one, and it is never too small or insignificant.

Question: How would you answer this question that comes up quite often for me, "Is this a pyramid?"

Answer: *I used to get asked this a lot as well, and what I came to realize is that the questions or the comments that led up to being asked this question were coming from me leading that person to think that this might be a scam, illegal, or one of those things.*

This is what I started doing when this was asked. I would turn it around and ask them, "Is there a reason you are thinking that?" You see there is a reason people ask you certain questions, and it typically comes from either prior experiences that they have had or the statements that you made to them before ask-ing, and check your pulse on this one, it could be that you think that too, so it's coming somewhere from within you.

In the beginning of my journey in the network marketing industry I thought everyone wanted to hear about the big mon-ey, because I was so excited about the big money. So I led with the conversation about big money, and I was using all those big-money words, such as you can make $10,000 a month with this, and you can do it quickly, and so many people are, which caused all the red flags to come up. So I stopped. I stopped leading with those types of comments or those types of questions, those types of remarks. And I stopped getting that type of question.

And then out of the blue, you could get asked. So here's a great answer. Simply say no. Just say no, and look at them. Because the last thing that you want to do is get into an argu-

ment or a discussion. I've learned to not take it personally or get defensive. Recognize that it is a legitimate question based on either prior remarks or from their experiences. So just respect it when they ask. And so when they ask, "Is it a pyramid?" you simply say no, and then just look at them. A lot of times they'll go, "Oh, okay." And then they might say, "Well, what makes this different? What makes this different than what would be called a pyramid?" Answer with highlights of who your company is and why you decided to partner with them along with a few minutes of your story. Keep it short and simple.

Don't be opposed to the question and don't get all wigged out or stumble around. Again, say no, and let the conversation evolve from there. As a side note, if there is something within you that perhaps you think that it's a pyramid because you're really not trusting it quite yet or you don't have the confidence that it works, then perhaps you need to do a little more due diligence on your company and catch a bigger vision. Start taking the products more regularly, getting the results that you want, and talk to leadership to get your belief level up. I can assure you that as time moves forward, you'll never hear that question again. I probably have not heard it since you just asked it for years.

Question: Why do people quit?

Answer: *Because they do. I used to wonder about this myself, because they join and pay money while being extremely excited, and then we are ghosted by them. I have found that it is really any number of reasons; however, I have also learned to let them go, because it could be that they never really initially wanted it, but on a whim they signed up. We have all done this on many* occasions. Sometimes they sign up and, within several weeks they are gone because a spouse or family member says something to them, and they were shocked and embarrassed by it, so they slide away without saying a word. They just disappear. It's as though they never existed. It used to blow me away, and I used to think, "Wow, wait a minute. What is wrong? What did I do wrong?" And then I would go back and answer that question. Is there anything that I could have done differently? And most of the time, 99 percent of the time, the answer was no, I did exactly with them as what I did with everyone else. I gave them the information they needed. I was there for them if they needed me. And so they just quit. They just quit.

So I started looking around at other industries. Let's take real estate for instance, you decide to become a real estate agent; therefore, you pay to take a test that you study for that's not easy to pass. Let's say you pass the test and get your real estate license. You start buying all the materials you need, such as business cards, signs, and so forth. You join a brokerage company and are willing to pay a fee to them and start advertising that you are now a real estate agent. Within a couple of months if you haven't sold a house, you give up. Let's look at all the boys who join Boy Scouts and never make it to Eagle. I bet it's less than 1 percent, and then what about sandlot football players that have big dreams of making it to the NFL but quit before they really give it everything they can. We don't even need to bring up the divorce rate, as we all know how many give up on this institution within a matter of a few months to a few years.

It's not just our industry that people quit. People quit life, people quit marriages, boyfriends, girlfriends, diets, workouts, and so forth. People give up very, very easily. And typically it's that 1 percent that are very persistent and that continue to learn *the necessary skills and gain the confidence as they go along the way that actually stay in and go to work and not give up on themselves and their dreams.*

How I overcame it myself was to not get bitter or discouraged. At first, I would get bitter if people quit perhaps for another company and took some of their team with them. I'm wondering why the heck would they do that? They were rocking it. They were really starting to get their rhythm down, starting to understand who they were, starting to gain their leadership skills. And they took off when it got a little bit tough, when maybe their check dipped a little bit, or they lost a rank. Maybe their team left because of reasons such as an illness in the family and life got a little too difficult, so they stepped away. I've got to step back a little bit. This hurts no matter what the reason is because you became friends and had this huge relationship. It can be heartbreaking. You start to question your own business when you know the business pays you, and the products are legitimate. You've met the corporate team, you love your upline, sideline, and downline. You love everything about it. But, because somebody else left, you start to question your own abilities and your own team and your own knowledge. So that's one of the things that we really need to guard. And that's our thoughts wrapped around other people quitting. They just quit for some reason. And a lot of times we will never find out the answer because they don't even know themselves. They start, something starts happening in their business, and they give up.

Maybe they just really can't take the leadership and they self-destruct. I've seen people get to a top-level position, and the heat is so high there and they feel so inadequate, but they would never acknowledge it. It's so subconscious that they don't take the time to look at themselves, to go within, and to get quiet and figure it out. Instead they look outside and they start to find things that are wrong. And I'm telling you, if you look hard enough, you're going to find stuff that you don't like just to take yourself out. It doesn't mean that they're real. You just will find it. I want you to go back and think about somebody that you dated. I mean, you were fine with them until you weren't, and then when you weren't, you started overanalyzing everything about them and the way they chewed gum bothered you. The way they walked bothered you when before you thought it was so cute. So, did they change? No, your idea of them did. And maybe it's just time to go, and that's okay.

So, people quit every single day for a lot of different reasons. Jim Rohn, a great mentor in this industry suggests that we don't take that class and try to figure out the reason. Just go, okay, they're gone. Now, let's move forward, because at the end of the day, you want to be the one standing. You want to be the strong one. You want to work through whatever's holding you back. And if you come across that idea of well, maybe it would just be easier to quit, I can assure you that it's not, the grass is truly not greener. It needs to be watered and nurtured and cared for where you're at. You can work through these thoughts, and see a lot of them are not true, they're just thoughts that come in because our ego wants to keep us at a certain level to feel safe. We must break free from that level, and that level could be a certain amount of money, it could be a certain amount of leadership, it could be any number of things as there are so many factors that can be involved that keep us stuck where we're at that we really need to look at and analyze. The most effective way that I have found to break through is by asking myself this very simple question, "Is that true about me?" I get really quiet and I answer it. If it's about the company, is that true about the company?

Does everybody feel that way or is it just that person? It's maybe something they need to work through because you don't want to give up on the business that you've created. You know, we've got people that left years ago, a decade ago, and if you look at their numbers, their down line, there's hundreds of thousands of potential dollars there that they just left on the table because they got scared about something or they got lazy or they didn't think it was working. Then, seventeen levels down here comes somebody that comes in and just starts to blow it away and just creates this massive business and you don't want to miss out on that.

I suggest staying the course and working through those negative thoughts that pop up. I work on myself, on my leadership, by reading, listening to the right people. Listen to the ones that are still doing the business in such a great way, in such a legitimate way, a way of integrity. Because when people leave, the thing that they want to do is take everybody with them, and they try very, very hard to do that, which hurts so many people and so many people's businesses. And I just don't want you to be that person. I believe so much in everyone and the skills that they have and what they can develop within themselves.

Question: How do you push out of the worst funk you've ever hit and come back stronger than ever when you feel like you have been hit hard and need to rebuild most of your business? I want this more than anything. I'm just a tad downtrodden at the moment and facing a ton of anxiety and stress. Please help.

Answer: *Thank you so much for being so open and honest. I truly love this question because at some point we've all been there, and we can go through this several times within our busi-*

ness because after all this is business, and it will always have its ups and downs. Nothing is ever just smooth sailing, so if we really take a great look at ourselves and our businesses, which it looks like you have, we will see that they correlate with our efforts, our desires, and our enthusiasm.

Now, when we slow down, our business does too. I used to wonder how the people on our team knew that I'd slowed down. I've taken myself out for a couple of weeks, and the team knew it because you just get quiet. It's like a hush goes over you and your business. They see that you post less, that you're reaching out to them less, and they start to question that. And before you know it, that trickles all the way through your organization. And we don't want to give anyone a reason to slow down. Now, I understand that life happens, and at times we have to step away and take care of life, but we can always stay connected and stay tapped into our team. So you're in a funk, the worst one ever. So how do you come back stronger?

There is no better way than just taking bold massive action. I don't know of any other way, but the action that is bold and massive needs to come from a place of fun and excitement and exuberance. It can't come from a place of desperation because right now I'm sensing a little bit of desperation because you're facing a ton of anxiety and stress. So that tells me that you're coming from a place of, "Oh my gosh, I'm about to lose my business. I've got to get it going. I don't even know where to turn. I don't feel good. I don't have the energy for it." So what we want to do is back up a little bit, reach down deep, and go back to why you originally started the business. What was it that caused you to want to join? What were you desiring? Why were you going after it in such a big way? Don't try to go back and figure out what happened and what took you out and what started causing the stress and anxiety. Don't try to figure that out. That's wasteful energy and wasteful time. The best thing you can do is get back in the game and get back in bigger than ever. And go back deep into that why—the reason that you started in the first place—get excited about it again. Get giddy, come back to your team, and be honest. Say, "Look, I don't know what happened to me. I went down a rabbit hole. I got lost. My desire left. And it was nothing other than a fickle brain. I have no idea why I did it, but I'm back stronger than ever, and I am here to help."

When you state this and feel this within you, then you can turn it around very quickly. You'll be surprised what will happen. You'll have people that will text you out of the blue. You'll have people come back to life. You'll have some people break away. Some people will say, "Oh, I liked it when she was quiet. I didn't have to work. Now she's back. I'm going to have to work. I don't want to work. I'm out." And that happens too.

But their thoughts of giving up were there all along. You just didn't realize it because you were so dormant and so quiet, and now they don't want it anymore. And that's okay too. You decide you can get this back and roaring by your actions based on enthusiasm, desire, and the willingness to get back into the game in a big way. And this may happen again throughout your career, and that's okay too. Not everybody is game on 100 percent of the time, and we think that they are, and we need to give ourselves a break and realize that at some point you probably got tired.

Something happened, and you sat down, and the next day you sat down again, and before you know it, weeks or months went by, and now you're looking back and going, "Whoa, where was I?" You can't even remember what took you out in the first place. So, just start having fun again, getting back out there in the game, taking that action because you know what to do. You *know how to sign up customers. You know how to sign up distributors. You know how to promote. Just start.*

Question: What is your opening conversation to start talking about the products when talking to someone online after giving them a compliment or comment?

Answer: *This is a great question, and this goes for those of us who are building both online and offline because there isn't a difference in the way a conversation should flow. After your compliment or comment, and this may go back and forth for a few conversations, because you don't want to come across as if that was the only reason you commented, then you can just sense when the timing is right for you to ask a lead-in question, such as, "Have you heard of such and such product?" Lead with whatever product you feel would be the one to ask them about. Let them respond back. Keep your answers short and to the point. Most importantly, don't answer a question that hasn't been asked. That's probably the biggest advice that I can give you. Allow it to play out.*

And then if you're offline, you know, for those of us who are out here every single day, we've got our samples or blitz cards with us. We either hand the card or sample over as we're starting a conversation with somebody, let's say you are at Target or Starbucks, and the clerk has done something nice for you; then you can give them a compliment such as, "Thank you so much for being so helpful today. I'd love to give you a coupon or sample of my product." Stop talking and hand them the sample or coupon, and give them the opportunity to look it over. Get very quiet. Keep that smile on your face. Let them look at it, let them read it, and once again, don't answer a question that hasn't been asked. Allow them the opportunity to ask you that first question, and then come back with a very short answer to the point with that smile on your face. Let them look at it a little longer. Ask another question. It just bounces back and forth. Now, because they're at work, they may not able to make an executive decision on purchasing right then. So you want to make sure that you contact them the best way that they want to be contacted, which could be Facebook, text messaging, Instagram, or whatever they offer. Know that your product line works for people, that you're excited about it so they can sense your enthusiam, and I promise you as you continue to do this, you're just going to get better and better.

Question: I'm having issues getting distributors and customers. I live in a touristy area in Maine, so in the winters many are unemployed and don't have the funds to do either. What is your advice on this?

Answer: *All right, we're going to totally change this up. Everybody thinks their area is the worst area for acquiring business. I have people here in Florida where it's sunny 90 percent of the time, and they say people aren't interested, and so it's coming from your perspective. If there's people in your area that don't have income, why wouldn't they be interested in an opportunity for more health or wealth? They would, so let's change it up. Let's change up your beliefs, and let's no longer say, "I'm having issues getting distributors or customers." Let's say instead, "I'm a recruiting machine, and everywhere I go people want my products and opportunity." You've got to switch up your belief and get your energy and excitement up.*

When you go out and you're feeling all those feelings, people can sense that you've got something going on. I remember a distributor coming up to me one time who said, "Pam, do I have a million-dollar bill on my forehead?" I said, "Why?" She said, "Because everywhere I go people are asking me about what I do. They're asking me these questions, and they don't know a thing about me. Now what was that?" That is a high energy of expectation and excitement. She was projecting that out to the world. People were sensing it, and they were wanting to be a part of whatever she had. What you may be doing, and this is subconscious, you may be projecting that nobody wants the opportunity or products. In other words, you are not expecting new business, and therefore, you aren't looking for it. You are not even asking.

Ask yourself these questions. Do I really want this to work? Am I excited? Am I taking the products and getting results? Make sure that you're using the products and that you're getting your own personal results so that you can go out there with more confidence and offer the products back out to the people that you talk to. And on the business side, whether you have made money or not, you've got to be excited about the possibilities. If you've got people in your area that, because it's wintertime, the market place is down, then they've got the time, they've got the desire to build something from home that they can work spare time, part-time. And so I would just acknowledge that and go out there with more exuberance, more energy, more excitement, and make sure that when you're talking to people, you really believe in what you're doing.

You can change your entire business by just really believing that it is possible. Saying, "Look, I know this works because I follow others that are making this happen. They believe in it, so I'll believe in it too." And then follow the people on Facebook or Instagram that you truly admire and listen to their stories as they continue to share them.

Question: What is the best way to inspire new distributors who don't live anywhere near me?

Answer: *In today's world being a global company with advanced technology, almost everyone's team members are not in the same area, especially since almost everyone builds online, this is a non-issue as far as distance is concerned; however, your question is one that I get asked most often because we all want a more motivated and inspired team. Most of us want ourselves to be more inspired. With new distributors it will be the stories of others that will help them catch a vision for themselves. I know for me when I started, I listened to the stories of other distributors and that motivated me to act. If it wasn't for these stories, I would not be here today. Find someone that your new distributor can relate to, perhaps with the same number of children or the same career, and introduce them so that they can see themselves and their future success through their story.*

Question: How do you keep from getting discouraged from all the noes and no responses?

Answer: *Noes have been a part of our life since we started hearing it from our parents, so what we must remember is that they have never hurt you other than perhaps your ego. It's typically what people say just to get you to stop asking them. Let's say you call someone, and they're having a regular day, and you ask them if they'd be interested in your products or your opportunity, and that was nowhere on their radar. You know, you're just* *coming in on a random day asking them one of those questions, and you're expecting a yes; well, more than likely you're not going to get it unless they're going through a phase of life called transition, and that transition could be like it was for my daughter Kaye, who grew up in the industry and was not interested until she was a senior in college and started realizing that very quickly she was going to have to go get a job. Kaye found herself in an upcoming transition of going from college student to employee. So she started paying attention to what I did and began asking me questions about the opportunity. She already loved the products but wanted more information on the business.*

You may contact someone who is in transition like Kaye was or you may not, but here's the thing: no means "not yet." You've planted a seed, and that seed was an ask of one of these two things, "Are you interested in taking a look at my products or my opportunity?" They may not be interested because at the time that you reached out to them their health may be perfection for them, but later they get a diagnosis or they want to lose weight because they've got a wedding to go to, and then they'll remember that you contacted them. So I never stopped contacting and checking in on the noes because I knew at any moment things can and do change.

Noes are a part of business and life; everyone goes through them and the way we overcome the thought of getting them and that feeling of rejection is just understanding this and asking anyway. I probably have received more noes than anyone else, and I haven't died from them, and neither will you. So just get up and understand that. Keep track of them knowing that at some point these noes may turn into yeses, and the more you receive, the bigger the business you will build.

Question: How do I push my team to work consistently without feeling like I am micromanaging them?

Answer: *As you probably know by now, no one likes to be micromanaged, and we certainly don't want to be pushed. What I sense from this question is frustration. We all want teams that want to get up and go to work and to be inspired. I learned this very early on by being observant of my very own thoughts. When I felt like my team needed pushing or motivating, I needed a push and I needed motivating because when I am on fire, then everyone around me is too. WOW! Let's really look at this question because it might the most important question ever asked. Our team is the direct reflection of what is going on within us right now. When we aren't consistent with our work by doing the things that promote us and drive our checks, then neither is our team. We unfortunately get lazy and want our teams to be inspired without us and go to work to increase our checks. Life and business don't work this way.*

Here's the secret. Go to work like your hair is on fire. Get a renewed desire that is so strong that you don't have time to see if your team is working or not. They will sense this in you and do one of two things, get to work or quit, and both are good. You will know who to play with and who to walk away from.

Question: How do I promote products I don't use? For instance, I don't drink coffee and I'm gluten free, so I can't use all the products.

Answer: *You know, that's okay if you don't; however, you know others that do. What we fail to realize is that life isn't all about us. It's about our potential customers, potential distributors, and what they're looking for. Get excited about that. Knowing* *that you have solutions for others, regardless of whether they are for you. For instance, you may not drink coffee; however, according to the latest coffee statistics from the International Coffee Organization, we pour about 1.4 billion cups of coffee a day worldwide.*

You simply share the testimonies of others using products that you're not currently using so that you have a vast array of testimonies. Don't feel like you must make something up. Don't feel like you're not telling the truth. Always lead with the truth, but find those other people within your team and organization or customers that are using some of these products, and you'll have success promoting them.

Question: I always had low self-esteem, but I really want to be successful with this business. How do I get past the deep-seated thought that I don't have what it takes?

Answer: *Remember this, if nothing else: you do have what it takes. How do I know this for sure? Because I have witnessed firsthand people that had extremely low self-esteem, anxiety, lack of confidence with very little belief in themselves gain their strength and confidence by doing the actual work. It doesn't happen by sitting around and wishing for it. It happens by the actual work. We all start out without any knowledge in almost every project or experience in life; however, the more we trust the process and get out in action, the more confidence we gain. Confidence comes by taking action. I think every single one of us could at some point in our life say we had low self-esteem, and it doesn't always go away. Sometimes it comes back in other areas. I know I've suffered from it in the past, and the only way that I* knew to get over it, because it's the only way that worked for me, was by the actual doing of whatever it is we want to accomplish.

Here's an example in my life. I felt a low self-esteem over getting back in the gym and exercising. For several years I didn't do any form of exercise, and when my daughter said she was going to have a baby, I thought, "Wow, I've got to be able to get up off the floor." I wanted to be stronger, more powerful. I went back in the gym with a very low self-esteem, and my confidence grew over time, and so did my results. It took effort, and many times I tried talking myself out of going, but I went and gained the results that I wanted.

So this is what I would recommend that you do: focus on your why. Why do you want this business to work for you? What are you looking for? What are the things that you want to get out of it? Then focus on those things. Don't focus on what you feel like you don't have, but focus on what you feel like you do have, and go after that. Over time, your self-esteem will grow as your business grows.

Question: I'm feeling defeated by the "I wanna order" that my potential customers are saying to me and they won't let me do it for them, so weeks later I've asked if they've had an issue with my site, and they say, "No, I just haven't done it yet." How do I deal with this?

Answer: *We've all done this, even to ourselves. Something is mentioned that my personal trainer will suggest that I order, and I'll tell him I'll do it right away; however, I get busy doing other things and totally forget about it.*

The best thing to do is be very honest with them and say, "If you are like me, you'll start doing something else and will forget about ordering and will miss getting these products that you want, so how about I get the information from you right now and let's get your order placed!" Then ask them for the specifics. Don't hesitate. Say, "What name will the account be in? What's the address?" and so forth. Take the order.

You know what happens? I'll tell people that I want something and that I'm going to order it. Even from Amazon. I'm working with someone in social media, and he's wanted me to order a tripod. Well, I'll go, "All right, I'll order it today," and I get home, and I get so busy, I forget about it when I should have just said, "Hey, fill up a cart, send it to me as a reminder, and then I'll order it."

Question: How are older distributors who aren't tech savvy able to build this business?

Answer: *They decide they want it. They decide that they're going to have fun, and they decide that they're going to stay in their gifts, they're going to use the gifts that they have and go build, and that's the way that I would do it if I started today. I feel like I'm a little tech savvy, but at times I'm not. However, let me tell you, I would go out and build a business in people's houses. I'd meet them one on one for coffee because you know what? I want the business to work. I want the rewards of a successful business, which is more income coming in. Friends I'm making all along the way, and people's lives are transforming by the opportunity and the products. It comes down to not mattering how you build but that you want the opportunity. There are online businesses and offline businesses. Both work today.*

Question: What's the best book to read for overcoming fear?

Answer: *You know, I don't know of one best book to offer; however, I would recommend that you Google "best books to read on fear" and see which one resonates with you.*

The very first book that I read in the self-development category was The Magic of Believing *by Claude Bristol. That book got me up off the couch and out to work and to go after my DREAMS. It wasn't a book just based on overcoming fear as it is a book about believing in yourself and believing that even if you are afraid, you can still do it.*

We are fearful most every day, but we work through it by the actions that we take. So fear tells me that I am going beyond where I am today and I embrace it. If we sit back comfortably and never are afraid, we're not evolving. We're not growing and neither is our business or our life. So embrace it. Know that you're headed somewhere great and that fear will crop up, but you'll be able to go right through it because you're going to have your why on what you want. You're going to feel capable that you can do it and you're going to overcome it every single moment by taking the necessary action steps.

Question: What are your non-negotiables every day for your business and personal life to keep your sanity, happiness, and to stay on track?

Answer: *It's nonnegotiable that I'm going to make up my bed every single day. It's the first thing that I do. I know that might sound silly to most people; however, it gets my day started in the right direction. It's nonnegotiable that I'm going to listen to or read something that moves me in the right direction. It's a nonnegotiable that I'm going to have coffee every single morning. It's* nonnegotiable that I'm going to do some form of exercise every single day. It's nonnegotiable that I'm going to eat right, take my supplements, and drink lots of water. It's nonnegotiable that I'm going to tell myself that I can be, do, and have everything that I want in life if I'm willing to go after it. It's nonnegotiable to pay attention to my inner dialogue and thoughts.

I feel like each of us should write down exactly what we're not willing to compromise in our life. I'm not willing to compromise giving up on my dreams. That's a nonnegotiable. I'm going to go after my dreams every single day. I'm going to build a strong viable business. I'm going to talk to anyone that is within a few feet of me about what we have to offer because I feel like if they're there, they're there for a reason, and they need to hear what we have to offer. I believe in it that much, so that's a nonnegotiable for me. You know, when you have a business that lives within you, you can't help but share it. If you have products that have literally changed the physical aspect of your body and how you feel, you can't help but share them. If a dream of yours has come true because of your business and your growth, you can't help but share it, so that's a nonnegotiable for me.

Another one is I'm going to hug and love on my family while being fully present. I'm going to spend as much time with them as I possibly can and let them know how much I care about and appreciate them. I'm going to take great care of my friends because I love them so much. They're a big part of my life, and most importantly beyond all of that and even within all of that, a nonnegotiable for me is I am going to have fun. If it's not fun, I am not going to do it. Life is meant to be joyful, and I want to live in that place of joy. Sometimes we must do things that at the time don't seem fun; however, I'm going to find the fun within them. I'm going to get myself geared up and go do it and find *something fun within it so that I don't feel like I'm wasting time and a nonnegotiable for me is I won't waste time. Time is such a precious commodity that I am going to spend every moment of every day fulfilling my life and the lives of those around me.*

Question: What are "we" having for breakfast?

Answer: *Ah, I love this question. We're going to have a great cup of coffee with chocolate greens and heavy cream whipped with a frothier, not stirred. I can pretty much fix anything for breakfast, so I'm going to let you pick that out. If you want bacon and eggs, girl, that's what we're going to have. If you want some gluten free, awesome pancakes, that's what we're going to have. If you want a shake, I'll fill it up with great greens, fruit, almond milk, and we're going to enjoy every moment of it as it comes out of that straw. Whatever you want, I'm willing to fix. I can't wait to have breakfast with you. And, the best part will be the conversation. That's always the best!*

Question: This is our second time around with the same company, and I really want to succeed this time; however, I am working full-time while going into the second year of being divorced, living paycheck to paycheck, paying for private high school, and maintaining a household for two very busy athletic teenage boys. I'm extremely busy with college applications, college visits, sporting events, and just daily life. This causes me to get sidetracked along with being tired and frustrated. By the time I sit down and work my business, I feel overwhelmed and don't know where to start and eventually end up not doing anything. How do I organize my days and weeks in order to ensure I am doing something great and productive to work my business?

Answer: *First, I admire you. I really, really do. You're a single mom, and you want more for yourself and your boys. There's always life, and I know if you can go back in your mind and remember that even when you were married, raising two young boys, there didn't seem to be enough time in the day. Most all of us come from places of too much busyness. And we use our children as reasons not to do it instead of the reasons to do it.*

If you don't make your business a priority in your life along with the reasons that you are doing it in the first place, then every day is going to be the same for you, a Groundhog Day. I would recommend that you make the decision that you are going to put this at the top of your list for top priority after your children and job. I would get up an hour early. Yes, you can do it if you really want this business to work. What I love about it is we are in the age of social media, which means we can work anytime and reach out and connect with people. Your time working doesn't have to be during working hours or even hours that most people are up. I would set a new routine. A routine for dreams and growth. Have your own power hour before the day begins for most people, and be as productive as you can in that hour. Be very focused and very intentional on what you want to accomplish, which is reaching out to people, following up with people, creating that big funnel of leads. And you know, I wish that I had had this opportunity with social media. We had to work the phones, that's all we had, and it had to be during hours where people would actually pick up the phone and answer it. So there really are no excuses.

Many times when we make up excuses, which seem very, very real and I'm not saying that these are not real, but these reasons cause us to procrastinate, which really means we're living in a place of fear, and we tend to not do the productive things that will grow our business. Are you living in fear? Are you procrastinating and not getting things done because you're thinking you're not going to get people on board. That people aren't going to respond to you. So get real with yourself, and answer those questions.

Question: Two of the leaders that I relied on have quit. I try and reach out to other distributors, but they reject me or do not answer me back when I'm asking for help or leadership. If we are one team, one mission, I'm not feeling it.

Answer: *There is no excuse or reason to rely on others for your success. We must look at our business as a business, and that it is our responsibility to learn what we need to learn and to plug into the people and systems that are available for us. There is so much information on different social media platforms that would take you years to watch.*

There are also others in the business just like you who have not connected with their "tribe." Ask around. Companies offer so many avenues for people to connect such as leadership group pages, events, Zooms, power hours, and so forth.

But let's also look at it from this viewpoint, you're going to be building a team, and your team is who you're going to really connect with, the people that you are sponsoring and bringing on board. This is about you building your own business and taking control of those reins and deciding, no matter if somebody is reaching out to me, I'm going to go after this, and I'm going to build my team. One of the best things that ever happened to me in the industry was my sponsor was not around. I had to dig around and figure out what the answers to the questions were. I had to read through the compensation plan to under-stand it, but it was the best thing that could have happened to me. I became self-sufficient—a leader. I didn't let it stop me, and I certainly didn't use it as an excuse.

This isn't an excuse as to why you shouldn't be building the business, and it doesn't sound like you are. It just sounds like you want to be connected. Again, you are going to find people out there to connect with as you build. Have fun, and enjoy the process.

Question: How do you seal the deal?

Answer: *Let's change that terminology from "seal the deal" to "ask from a place of sharing." I know that you are asking, "How do I close? How do I get people to buy? How do I get distributors to join?" If we can change our terminology from sealing the deal and just become awesome at building relationships and answer-ing people's questions and being inspiring, then basically what we do is we just ask in a very bold way questions such as this, "What do you see yourself doing? Do you see yourself becoming a customer or do you see yourself becoming a distributor?" In other words, just ask. This is the biggest thing that I see, that distributors simply don't ask their potentials what they would like to do. We all want to buy, we just don't want to be sold.*

It's no different than going in and purchasing a car. How would it feel to go in and the salesman that is helping you and guiding you never asks, "What would it take for you to purchase this car?" They are always asking and asking and asking. And that's one thing that we don't do enough of is really getting down to that ask. And this is the biggest thing that I see for people because they're afraid they're going to get rejected. I would rather get a no than just hang out there waiting for the customer or the potential distributor to come back to me. I want you to be bold. I want you to go for the ask and go big and go back to everybody that you've ever talked to and say, "Hey, I'm just wondering where you're at. Are you ready to become a part of my team? I just see something great in you." Or, "Hey, are you ready to be a customer? You stated that you wanted to lose some weight and that you want to get healthy." Just ask some great questions, and don't feel like you're sealing a deal. That's not what we're doing here. We are offering a tremendous benefit to people either on the customer side or the distributor side. So change up that verbiage a little bit and be bold and ask those vital questions so that your business can take off and head in the direction that you want to go.

Question: How do you keep your team motivated and when is too much help for them? I have a Team Page, Zooms, Parties, and help him in every way, yet it seems like no matter what I do some get so close to promotions and stop. Is there something I'm missing to make them push harder?

Answer: *Well, for one thing, getting people to push harder will turn into them pushing away. It's almost impossible to motivate people and to motivate teams for very long, but we can inspire them by our own work. It sounds to me that you feel like you're pushing and pulling people along and perhaps doing way too much for them. I would recommend that you spend 80 percent of your time developing new team members and 20 percent* *of your time working with those that are doing all the things, which is bringing in new team members and new customers. When your team sees new team members come on board directly connected to you, they're going to do one or two things: either they're going to want that for themselves or they're just going stay where they're at and not do anything.*

Biggest lesson I think all of us have learned over the years or decades that we've been in this industry is we can't do it for people and we certainly can't motivate them, but we can inspire them by them seeing exactly what we're doing and that is with our daily actions of being persistent in what truly makes us money.

I would make the decision that your focus is all in on your own business right now, that you're going to go ahead and put in new people, whether it's customers or distributors, and you are going to have fun and you're not going to try and motivate anybody. They're going to be so inspired to be a part of what you're building that they're going to go get new people on their own and you're going to start to see those charts fill up and those promotions take place.

Question: This past year was my first-year anniversary in the industry, and I'm just getting started and have had one promotion so far. More than anything, I want to become a better leader. How do I do that?

Answer: *Since you are still new in the industry and have experienced a promotion, I know you would like your focus to be on leadership; however, your focus should be on building. That is really what it means to lead. A leader is one who is leading by doing the work, which means they are bringing in new team* members and training them on how to get started. As you do this, you will experience moments when you need some help in leading people through the process; however, this comes with the "doing" of the business and not by reading or listening to something. It's like the horse before the cart. You've got to fill up the cart.

Once you start building a larger team then read books on leadership and listen to incredible people, whether it's through podcasts such as the Pam Sowder Podcast or going on YouTube and listening to anything by Jim Rohn, who was an industry leader and trainer.

However, nothing is better than experience, so as your business grows, you're going to do some things that later on you will look back at and ask yourself, "Why did I do that?" which means you are gaining wisdom. I have found the best wisdom that I've gained is from working with people and not necessarily the books that I've read or the tapes that I've listened to. It's being in daily tasks and understanding the different personalities of people while making sure that I am really listening to them so that I can find out what their needs are. Listening is essential in leadership. The skills come as we grow our business, so grow a huge business, and you will become an outstanding leader along the way.

Question: I was in the business for five years and had one promotion while working the business 24/7. I wanted to promote several more ranks and still do, but I feel that my problem was in those five years I was always on work mode, so I got burnout and left and just recently came back. I'm scared because I think I won't make it. I don't want to get into the overdrive desperation mode again just to go nowhere. Most importantly, I want a quality of life while being with my babies and to teach my team that they can have the same. Please help.

Answer: *Oh my gosh, this is one of my favorite questions. So let's deep-dive into this because I've got a few red flags that I'm reading here, and the first one is that you say you worked your business 24/7 for five years. I know that if that were the case you should have promoted several ranks within those five years unless of course the work was unproductive. This is a question that only you can answer. I know that if I am doing the productive work of putting in new customers and distributors and leading my team, I would have promoted within five years all the way to the top as do most people. I see a lot of people who think that they are working when they are on Facebook or Instagram; however, they're scrolling, scrolling, scrolling, or they're reading things, listening to You Tube training videos, but nothing's moving because the work isn't the productive work, the work that produces new customers and distributors.*

Take a strong look at what you're doing every day, and see how much time you're wasting just scrolling, looking, reading, and watching other people. I know that there are mentors in the business that you admire who are at the promotion that you want to achieve. Most have a very active family life and they do all the things. This doesn't mean that on occasion they don't feel stress or tired, which they know then to kick in some "me" time.

The best thing that I do for myself is set my own daily schedule. I fill my day with what I want to accomplish, and I don't waste precious time with unproductive habits. I would suggest you take an inventory of your current days and see where you should implement some changes. Nothing will change unless you change. I know you can have it all because so many have.

Lastly, the feeling of desperation comes from a place of desiring something so much that you are willing to do whatever it takes to get there; however, because it comes from desperation, you will therefore always be desperate. This again is a deep dive into self-development. Read and listen to books, podcasts, and the leaders that you admire to develop yourself so that you come from a place of prosperity that there is enough time, people, and money to go around without sacrificing any part of your life.

Question: I want to advertise on TV, plus Internet, and in a kiosk space. I could use some help getting it set up. I tried this once at a wrong location, but I have another one that is awesome. Please let me know what you think.

Answer: *I love your enthusiasm for all of this and would recommend this to you, but TV and Kiosk space is not our jam. Our marketing vehicle is through independent distributors and not through other forms of media; however, I don't want to curtail your excitement. Advertising (sharing) online through social media platforms are working for our teams.*

I would recommend that you learn to work your business from home and look into attending events such as trade shows and things like that where you can set up a booth and get people interested in trying the products or the opportunity. This will save you time and money. Our business model is direct sales, which gives you leverage with your time, sales, and knowledge. We each order a few products every month, and we teach other people to do the same thing. We keep it simple and duplicate.

Question: I really wish this would work for me. I just don't know what to do. I've tried everything and nothing's working.

Answer: *I too thought this when I first got started in the industry. However, I started observing the actual work of other leaders who were successful and realized that I was just wishing that it would work. The work that I put in was not the work that caused your business to grow; it was just busy work. So I will base my answer on my own experience and being asked this multiple times in the last few decades. It's going to get real, so make sure you are sitting down.*

It's called networking, not netwishing. We just gotta get to work. That's the number one thing. You know, I used to just wish, wish, wish, and when people tell me that they've tried everything and talked to everybody, I know that's not true because you can't say the right thing to the wrong person. You can't say the wrong thing to the right person. So simply it's a numbers game. I wish there was more to it than that. I wish there was a magic formula. Here we go back to that word wish*. I wish there was a magic statement, a magic post, a magic ask but there isn't; it's called work, and it's the best kind of work when you catch the vision of what you really want and believe that it can happen.*

Think about it. You get to choose when and where you work, how long you work, and who you work with—not to mention the unlimited income that is available. That's a beautiful thing. So let's take advantage of what we already have and what we already know and realize that it's going to take more than just contacting a handful of people. It takes commitment, persistence, and desire. So let's get back to why you signed up in the first place. What were you wishing for? What do you want? And get really clear. Get really, really clear about why you decided to be a part of this industry and start a home-based business. This is the most vital thing when people are wishy-washy and say, "Oh, I want $10,000 a month." I know that that's not true.

Yeah, they'd like to have it if it were handed to them, but they're not willing to go work for it. There's a difference because when you truly desire that $10,000 a month, you don't need to say it, you just go do it. You put your head down, you stay focused, nothing or no one can take you out, and you get the job done. And very few of us understand that and realize that this is not a wishing business. This is a working business, and it will fulfill all your wishes if you work it along the way. So what do you do? You decide. Make a strong decision that you're going to go after it. All right, this is what I want, why I want it, and I'm willing to decide right here, right now, and go after it.

So then start. Make the list of all the people that you know and don't prejudge them. Have a hundred names, two hundred names, as many as you can, and every day add to that list. Posting alone on social media is not asking. You have to be bolder than that. You must go in behind the scenes and the facade of your social media newsfeed and truly ask people or however you normally interact with people should be the way that you approach them about the business.

When you have that strong desire and it's backed with your why, people can sense it. They know there's something different about you. They can't put their finger on it, but they know just by the way that you're carrying yourself, the energy that's coming from you, the way that you voice something, that something's different about you, and it gets them curious.

They start to wonder what's going on, what does she have? And they might even start asking you questions. But when you don't, when you're wishing and you're wondering and you're not confident and your why is not strong, you're just kind of throwing things out there, hoping somebody bites and when they don't, you're like, I'm good. I'm out. That's netwishing. Networking is when you make a conscious decision that no matter what happens, I'm going to keep going. I'm going after what's on my dream board. I'm going after my big why. So you start, you make the list, you start asking, you can ask in several different ways. You can just be bold and out front and say, "I thought about you, you'd be awesome in my business. Are you open to looking at it?" That's it. Start there and network!

Question: I have been in the industry for two years, and while I am excited about the rank that I have attained, I want to go to the next level; however, I'm going to need to rebuild as most of my team is not working. How do I get over the fact that I have team members who are still in but just sitting there? I care about them, but I also know I need to wipe the slate clean and start with some fresh people so I can move forward. I'd love your thoughts on wiping the slate clean and starting with fresh people without hurting the ones that I have.

Answer: *It's one of the hardest things that I remember going through myself because you enjoy working with your team; however, they are not growing or evolving and let's be real, you probably became inactive with them. When we use the word rebuild we at some point stopped building or we would not have a need to say it. I knew that I had sat down with my team and expected them to continue without realizing that they are following my every move, so when I'm not moving, the team is not moving.*

So now what? Start. Where are you charting to next? Get that roadmap out and ask your team who is going with you. Some will and some won't, but you've got to find out who they are and quickly. Once this is known, then everyone is going af-

ter their next promotion, and you will see who really means it very quickly; however, your main vision and work is on your next promotion. Once you cast this vision for yourself and your team, then you must start bringing in new team members, and your team needs to do the same. The work is always the same; however, you can create massive momentum once your mind is made up of where you are going next. Stick to the vision and don't stop until you get there, and this time once you achieve, you are immediately going after the next promotion because you don't want to get back into complacency and you and your team stall out again.

Question: I just promoted to the 2nd rank position and I've been struggling with self-discipline, training new team members, sufficiently keeping track of my business and making sure I'm available to them. How do you structure your time so that you can divide in so many places?

Answer: *You know, this is a great question. I've answered this in so many different ways over the last couple of years. One of the beautiful things about being an entrepreneur is that you get to set your own schedule. Your team is young in growth and numbers, so it is important that you start this habit early on. Sit down and decide what hours you want to work and when you want to work them.*

When are you going to be available for your team, and when are you going to be available for your own business? You get to set that time so that way your team knows when they can ask you questions and when you're going to answer. Now they can ask you questions all day long, but you're only going to answer them in that allotted window that you've scheduled out. The rest of the time which is approximately 80 percent you want to be working on new business.

If you've got three hours scheduled for your business daily, 80 percent of those three hours should be acquiring new customers and distributors so that you can continue to grow your check. Your current team members should be plugged into an upline team page where they can find the solutions to their questions along with training videos they can learn from. Keep in mind that most people that are going to go after this business are very self-sufficient and will find the answers for themselves. Spend most of your time recruiting new and then guiding everyone else on how they can find their own answers. That's the best form of duplication.

About the Author

Pam Sowder

Pam Sowder is the Co-Founder of It Works!, a multi-million dollar network marketing company that's been changing lives since 2001 in over twenty countries.

Pam has been voted one of the most influential women in direct selling and has earned the nickname "Queen." She has over two decades of experience in direct sales and was an original brand ambassador and influencer. Pam has empowered tens of thousands of people to turn their dreams into reality at trainings and conferences around the world. Through her experience she realized that the "rich" girls often started as the "poor" girls in more ways than just financial. The "rich" girls realized their self-worth and rose to their potential, got over themselves and what was holding them back, and most importantly, achieved lasting success while having fun. Pam is not a guru, but what she's good at is getting you to say "AHA!"